Defeating the Jihadists

The Century Foundation expresses its appreciation to PublicAffairs for its assistance in the editing and preparation of this report.

This report was commissioned by The Century Foundation as part of its major Homeland Security Project. The project began with a working group cochaired by former Governors Thomas Kean and Richard Celeste. Some components of the project are supported in part by the John S. and James L. Knight Foundation, the Carnegie Corporation of New York, the Robert Wood Johnson Foundation, and the John D. and Catherine T. MacArthur Foundation. The task force was assembled and chaired by Richard A. Clarke. More information on this project can be found at www.homelandsec.org or The Century Foundation's main Web site, www.tcf.org.

DEFEATING THE JIHADISTS

A Blueprint for Action

The Report of a Task Force Assembled and
Chaired by RICHARD A. CLARKE
GLENN P. AGA, ROGER W. CRESSEY,
STEPHEN E. FLYNN, BLAKE W. MOBLEY,
ERIC ROSENBACH, STEVEN SIMON,
WILLIAM F. WECHSLER, LEE S. WOLOSKY

The Century Foundation

THE CENTURY FOUNDATION PRESS ◆ NEW YORK

The Century Foundation sponsors and supervises timely analyses of economic policy, foreign affairs, and domestic political issues. Not-for-profit and nonpartisan, it was founded in 1919 and endowed by Edward A. Filene.

Library of Congress Cataloging-in-Publication Data

Defeating the Jihadists : a blueprint for action / by Richard A. Clarke, chair ... [et al.].
p. cm.
"A Century Foundation report."
Includes bibliographical references.
ISBN 0-87078-492-7 (hardcover: alk. paper) -- 0-87078-491-9 (pbk.: alk. paper)
1. Terrorism--Government policy--United States. 2. Terrorism--United States--Prevention. 3. Terrorism--Islamic countries. 4. Jihad. 5. United States--Foreign relations--Islamic countries. 6. War on Terrorism, 2001- I. Clarke, Richard A. II. Century Foundation. III. Title.

HV6432.D436 2004
363.32'0973--dc22 2004025180

Cover design and illustration: Claude Goodwin

10 9 8 7 6 5 4 3 2 1

Foreword

The public and experts alike generally reacted to the collapse of the Soviet Union with a sense of optimism about the future—an optimism built upon a firm belief in America's global preeminence and near invulnerability. This consensus went largely unchallenged despite the fact that most scholars, analysts, and officials had been disquietingly off base in failing to foresee the end of the Cold War. Of course, concern about the shortcomings of intelligence analysts and security scholars was blunted by the fact that the "unexpected" news turned out to be very good news indeed. Regrettably, the luxury of such complacency about American invincibility turned out to be all too brief an experience. The events of September 11, 2001, wrenched the nation and the world into a stark realization that peace and security remained fragile and the threat of terrorism had been widely underestimated.

Inside the U.S. government, however, the seriousness of this threat had been identified well before September 11, albeit by a relatively small group of professionals. They had become increasingly convinced during the 1980s and early 1990s that new dangers to the United States and Europe were a growing possibility. They worked to increase the security focus of governments on terrorism, especially on the threat posed by would-be jihadists who saw the United States and its allies as the principal impediment to their dreams of radical and fundamentalist Islamic states. As the work of the 9/11 Commission has shown, while most of us lost our moorings in the immediate aftermath of the attacks on the World Trade Center and the Pentagon, these individuals had a clear understanding of the enemies we faced and the policies we needed to fight them.

Among this group are the authors of this report: Glenn P. Aga, Richard A. Clarke, Roger W. Cressey, Stephen E. Flynn, Blake W. Mobley, Eric Rosenbach, Steven Simon, William F. Wechsler, and Lee S. Wolosky.

These authors are a remarkable group, rich in experience, scholarly in the depth of their knowledge, and practical in the relevance of their prescriptions. In their report, they draw on their immense store of knowledge and experience, providing a taut description of the most important terrorist groups operating today and offering candid and concise descriptions of the political and security circumstances of the Muslim nations that are absolutely essential for a successful strategy to combat terrorism. And, perhaps most important, the authors of *Defeating the Jihadists: A Blueprint for Action* have charted a course for a more effective response to the threat of terrorism.

Almost fifteen years ago, The Century Foundation began a series of projects concerned with the need to reorient intelligence efforts after the end of the Cold War. In 1993, following the bombing of the World Trade Center, we intensified these efforts, producing two task force reports along the way, *The Need to Know* and *In From the Cold.* After September 11, we launched a significant expansion of related work, beginning a major Homeland Security Project cochaired by former Governors Thomas Kean and Richard Celeste and supported by the John S. and James L. Knight Foundation, the Carnegie Corporation of New York, the Robert Wood Johnson Foundation, and the John D. and Catherine T. MacArthur Foundation. Numerous publications have been produced as part of this project, including a report on the need for a Department of Homeland Security, a paper on security challenges facing state and local governments, and a book of essays, *The War on Our Freedoms.* This task force was assembled and chaired by Richard A. Clarke. The Century Foundation's Homeland Security Project is ongoing in the hope of provoking more discussion of alternative strategies for the effort to contain terrorism.

Wherever one comes out on the efficacy of recent policy, different choices are possible and debate is desirable. This volume is premised on the notion that we will be better prepared for the tests ahead if we are a nation armed not just with a powerful military and well-organized intelligence apparatus but also with a deeper public understanding of what we are up against and what we need to do. The thoughtful analysis in this report reminds us that, when making policy, ideology is no substitute for expertise, thorough knowledge, and thoughtful reflection. Since September 11, much has been done, but no one can promise an end to risk. In the struggle against terrorism, the United States and its allies have sufficient power, wealth, and patriots to force compliance with our wishes, at least for a time, upon most other nations. But our strength is not unlimited. We must use it with wisdom and efficiency. Otherwise, we shall squander opportunities for greater security and erode essential support from our own people and our allies. No course seems certain to lead to a quick diminution of the dangers we face. While any long-term strategy will test our patience and resolve, it is becoming increasingly clear that we must begin by sweeping away many misconceptions about our enemies and redressing any existing misallocation of our resources. To some extent, we must reorient our debate about what to do, founding it on a deeper understanding of the threat and a stronger commitment to developing a global coalition to combat it.

The authors of this report have done a great service by laying out the facts about the dangers we face and the realities of future policy choices. On behalf of the Trustees of The Century Foundation, I thank them for their efforts.

RICHARD C. LEONE, *PRESIDENT*
The Century Foundation
October 2004

Contents

Task Force Members

Richard A. Clarke served the past three presidents as special assistant to the president for global affairs, national coordinator for security and counterterrorism, and special adviser to the president for cybersecurity. Prior to his White House years, he served for nineteen years in the Pentagon, the intelligence community, and the State Department. During the Reagan administration, he was deputy assistant secretary of state for intelligence. During the George H. W. Bush administration, he was assistant secretary of state for political-military affairs and coordinated diplomatic efforts to support the 1990–91 Gulf War and the subsequent security arrangements. He is the author of *Against All Enemies: Inside America's War on Terror* (Free Press, 2004) and is a consultant to ABC News.

Glenn P. Aga is president and cofounder of IC Associates, LLC, advising U.S. government and corporate clients on a wide range of security issues and technologies. He is a former U.S. Air Force intelligence officer with overseas crisis experience in the Middle East, Africa, and the Balkans. He also served in the Clinton White House, the National Reconnaissance Office, the Office of the Secretary of Defense, and the State Department's Bureau of Intelligence and Research. He has supported and applied technology for counterterrorism operations and UN peacekeeping operations and has served as an analyst on global chemical and biological weapons capabilities.

Roger W. Cressey is president of Good Harbor, advising clients on homeland security, cybersecurity, and counterterrorism issues. He is currently an on-air counterterrorism analyst for NBC News. Previously, he served as director for transnational threats on the National Security Council staff, where he was responsible for coordination and implementation of U.S. counterterrorism policy. During this period, he managed the U.S. government's response to the millennium terror alert, the USS *Cole* attack, and the 9/11 attacks. Prior to his White House service, he served in the Department of Defense, including as deputy director for war plans. From 1991 to 1995, he served in the Department of State working on Middle East security issues. He also has served overseas with the U.S. Embassy in Israel and with UN peacekeeping missions in Somalia and the former Yugoslavia. While in the former Yugoslavia, he was part of a UN team that planned the successful capture of the first individual indicted for war crimes in Croatia.

STEPHEN E. FLYNN is the Jeane J. Kirkpatrick Senior Fellow for National Security Studies at the Council on Foreign Relations. He is a retired U.S. Coast Guard commander and an expert on homeland security and border control. He recently served as director and principal author for the task force report *America—Still Unprepared, Still in Danger* (Council on Foreign Relations, 2002), cochaired by former Senators Gary Hart and Warren B. Rudman. He has written extensively on security issues, including his recent book, *America the Vulnerable: How Our Government Is Failing to Protect Us from Terrorism* (HarperCollins, 2004).

BLAKE W. MOBLEY is a doctoral candidate specializing in counterterrorism and international relations at Georgetown University.

ERIC ROSENBACH is a national security consultant for the Belfer Center for Science and International Affairs at Harvard University. He previously served four years as a military intelligence officer supporting operations in the Balkans. He is a former Fulbright Scholar who studied law at Georgetown and public policy at Harvard.

STEVEN SIMON specializes in Middle Eastern politics at the RAND Corporation. Previously, he served in London for three years as assistant director of the International Institute for Strategic Studies and Carol Deane Senior Fellow in U.S. Security Studies. He came to the IISS in November 1999 from the National Security Council staff at the White House, where he served for more than five years as director for global issues and senior director for transnational threats. During this period he had coordination responsibilities for Near Eastern and South Asian security policy and counterterrorism policy and operations. He is coauthor of

The Age of Sacred Terror (Random House, 2002), which won the Council on Foreign Relations 2004 Arthur Ross Award, and coeditor of *Iraq at the Crossroads: State and Society in the Shadow of Regime Change* (Oxford University Press/IISS, 2003).

William F. Wechsler has held a number of senior government positions including: special advisor to the secretary of the Treasury, director for transnational threats at the National Security Council, and special assistant to the chairman of the Joint Chiefs of Staff. During his years in government, he led U.S. efforts to combat international money laundering, chaired the interagency effort to disrupt Osama bin Laden's financial network, and coordinated the drafting of Presidential Decision Directives on political-miliary planning for complex contingencies, on managing international civilian police operations, and on defending American computer networks and critical infrastructures from information warfare. He received his BA from Cornell University and a Master's Degree from Columbia University's School of International and Public Affairs. He is currently a vice president of Greenwich Associates, the international financial services strategic consulting firm and is a CFA charterholder.

Lee S. Wolosky is of counsel at Boies, Schiller & Flexner LLP and adjunct professor in international affairs at Columbia University. He served as director for transnational threats on the National Security Council under Presidents Bill Clinton and George W. Bush. His responsibilities included coordinating White House policy formulation, program oversight, and new initiatives related to international crime, including illicit finance affecting national security.

1. OVERVIEW

The primary national security challenge confronting the United States in the immediate future and likely for the next generation will be the international jihadist terrorism network. Members of that movement are a small minority of the Muslim world who seek to overthrow governments based upon a perverted interpretation of Islam.

Governments and the media use the phrase "al Qaeda" or "al Qaeda–related" to describe the network of jihadist terrorist groups. Despite the U.S. invasion of Afghanistan and the arrests of jihadist leaders around the world, the jihadist network remains strong. It has conducted twice as many attacks since September 11, 2001, as it did in the three years prior to that date. Jihadist leaders who have been captured or killed have been replaced. Although it is difficult to be precise about the number of active jihadists, the strong consensus among experts is that the ranks of the jihadists have increased significantly since 9/11.

Since 9/11, President George W. Bush's administration has squandered valuable time in addressing the jihadist threat. As we evaluate U.S. progress in neutralizing the jihadist movement, we need to acknowledge that the war in Iraq has been deeply counterproductive to the greater effort.

As a sin of commission, the Iraq war alienated crucial allies in the battle against jihadists, made friendly Muslims into skeptics, turned skeptics into radicals, and created a new battleground for itinerant jihadist insurgents. Iraq had no connection to the terror threat facing the United States, and Saddam Hussein's removal has done nothing to lessen the threat we face from al Qaeda and the jihadists. Perhaps the most vivid demonstration of this point is that more than a year and a half after Saddam's removal, the terror alert level in America remains elevated and there is anticipation of a major al Qaeda attack. The simple fact is that even if Iraq magically turned into a stable, secure democracy one day, the United States could suffer another 9/11-type attack the next day.

As a sin of omission, the Iraq war diverted massive and much-needed resources from the war on jihadists. The continued unrest in Iraq will further delay any U.S. effort to create a new international coalition to confront Syria's and Iran's terrorist activities. The international consensus to confront state sponsors of terrorism evaporated as a result of the Iraq war, a point not lost on Damascus and Tehran. As a result, they will do everything in their power to further bog down U.S. efforts in Iraq. Ironically, the war in Iraq has contributed to creating the breathing room Syria and Iran so desperately needed to avoid a robust international response to their terrorist activities.

The reliance on U.S. contractors to rebuild Iraq has slowed the reconstruction and restoration of services. U.S. contractors and their foreign subcontractors are unable to move freely about the country due to security concerns. The lack of services has, in turn, added support for the insurgency and the terrorist network. To accelerate the reconstruction and to give more responsibility to the Iraqi government, the United States should change its aid and procurement rules and procedures to give more of the U.S. money directly to the Iraqi authorities. There is a risk of corruption in this idea, but there is also a risk of mismanagement with U.S. companies.

In an effort to have a nationwide election in January 2005, the U.S. authorities plan a series of attacks on "no go zones" where insurgents have taken control of large urban areas. Such attacks will be counterproductive, with high collateral damage. For long-term stability, the United States should contain movement in and out of the insurgent areas rather than engaging in urban combat that will alienate those in the cities and those who watch the fighting on television in the Islamic world.

We can be lulled into thinking that we are making good progress in quelling the jihadists by noting that many positive things have happened since 9/11. We have disrupted the central al Qaeda organization. Many of its leaders have been captured or killed (and replaced). There has been greater international cooperation on terrorist financing in the international banking system, although that has only forced the money flow into the underground financial markets. Some homeland security initiatives have begun to address vulnerabilities, but most weaknesses remain largely unchanged.

The war against the jihadists must be, and can still be, won. This report provides a blueprint for succeeding in that enormous challenge. The 9/11 Commission provided its own excellent road map, which we endorse; our analysis seeks to build on its recommendations.

The task of defeating the jihadists has four important components, which will be examined herein:

- capturing or killing the hard-core terrorists who are intent upon murder and martyrdom,
- improving relations with the Islamic world and with specific nations therein, to reduce support for the jihadists,
- reducing America's vulnerabilities to terrorist attack at home and abroad, and
- reinventing or transforming government services and capabilities to support the three tasks above.

Other related issues of equal importance and difficulty must be addressed to defeat the jihadists. They are complicated but essential challenges that deserve detailed treatment elsewhere but are touched on in this report only briefly to suggest their relevance and a general direction for analysis. Due to the lack of significant progress in the last decade, they too must be pursued with unusual speed:

- reducing the threat from the proliferation of nuclear weapon and biological weapon technologies, and
- shifting the economy from dependence on foreign fossil fuel sources for energy requirements.

In pursuing all of these objectives, the nation would benefit greatly from developing clear measurements of progress to assist the public in judging whether adequate success is being achieved. Both the media and Congress bear responsibility for monitoring such measurements and promoting continuing debate on the efficacy of efforts to address those challenges.

This report suggests a broad and comprehensive strategy. It begins with a description of the threat and how it has changed, providing details about the many groups that make up the jihadist movement.

Adding to the recommendations of the 9/11 Commission, the analysis here suggests the need for detailed country strategies for increasing stability in Egypt, Saudi Arabia, Pakistan, Iran, and Iraq. It also proposes: (1) taking an active anti-jihadist approach to the Islamic world in general; (2) developing enhanced counterterrorism capabilities in our intelligence, anti-terrorist financing, law enforcement, and military communities; and (3) improving our homeland security capabilities, securing nuclear weapons technology and materials around the globe, and developing a plan to attain energy independence for the United States.

The Report's Key Recommendations

Clarify the Threat: To be effective, we must have consensus about the nature of the problem facing us. It should be clarified that the threat is not terrorism, or even all terrorist organizations, but rather the jihadist terrorists who seek to hijack Islam and use violence to replace existing governments with nondemocratic theocracies.

Engage in the Battle of Ideas: In addition to countering the jihadist terrorists with law enforcement, intelligence, and military measures, we must erode support for them in the Islamic world through what the 9/11 Commission called the "Battle of Ideas." Nations other than the United States (including both Islamic and non-Islamic countries) and nongovernmental organizations must take the lead in actively appealing to Muslims to denounce intolerance and terrorist violence conducted in the name of Islam. These efforts must stress our common values and overcome misunderstandings and terrorist propaganda. Reactivating the Israel-Palestine peace process must be a part of this larger effort. As part of the Battle of Ideas, the United States and Europe must demonstrably welcome Islam as a part of their cultures. For Europe, it is essential to fight anti-Islamic discrimination in European Union member countries; it is equally important that EU member states be willing to approve formal entry talks paving the way for Turkey's accession to the EU. Both the European Union and the United States need a concerted program to fight religious intolerance against Islam.

Provide Assistance to Islamic Nations: Although jihadist terrorists are often not poor or uneducated, they use the underprivileged populations in some Islamic nations as one base for their support and as a lever for undermining national stability. The United States, the European Union, wealthy Arab states, and the international financial institutions must greatly expand their financial and programmatic support for development efforts in Afghanistan, Uzbekistan, Pakistan, Yemen, Jordan, Morocco, and other economically challenged Islamic nations. These efforts must support human rights efforts and strengthen educational systems and economic opportunities, especially for women.

IMPLEMENT TAILORED STRATEGIES FOR KEY COUNTRIES: The United States must have tailored, detailed, proactive, and integrated policies for enhancing stability and democratic forces in key Islamic nations, including Iran, Pakistan, Saudi Arabia, Egypt, and Iraq. As part of this effort, the United States must develop its own reliable sources of information about domestic political, social, and security trends in these nations.

DEFUSE SOURCES OF ISLAMIC HATRED FOR THE UNITED STATES: The jihadist terrorists oppose the United States not for what it believes or does, but because they see America as a barrier to their creation of theocratic nation-states or caliphates. Many supporters of the jihadists, however, are persuaded to oppose the United States and support the terrorists because of specific U.S. actions and policies, especially America's support for Israel and occupation of Iraq. The United States should not alter its support of Israel, but it should seek to revivify the Israel-Palestinian peace process. The United States should not precipitously withdraw from Iraq before indigenous security forces are in place but should cease U.S. military operations against urban areas, transfer rebuilding activities to Iraqi entities, abandon the concept of permanent U.S. military bases in the country, and reduce U.S. goals in Iraq so that a withdrawal can be achieved at an early date.

IMPROVE U.S. INTELLIGENCE AND LAW ENFORCEMENT ORGANIZATION: In addition to speedily implementing the recommendations of the 9/11 Commission, the United States should modify personnel policies in intelligence and law enforcement agencies (notably the Central Intelligence Agency and Federal Bureau of Investigation) to facilitate noncareer tracks. The domestic intelligence activities of the FBI should be performed by a distinctly separate new organization within the bureau. The next administration should establish an independent, outside oversight board, as recommended by the 9/11 Commission, rather than the internal advisory group recently created by executive order.

ELIMINATE TERROR FINANCING: The next president should designate a special assistant to the president for combating terrorist financing at the National Security Council, with the specific mandate to lead U.S. efforts on terrorist financing issues. Congress should pass and the president should sign legislation requiring the executive branch to submit to

Congress on an annual basis a written certification detailing the steps that foreign nations have taken to cooperate with American and international efforts to combat terrorist financing.

IMPROVE U.S. MILITARY ORGANIZATION: The U.S. military's special operations forces for counterterrorism activities should be greatly expanded and should be supported by a military organization that maintains a covert—"not official cover"—presence in other nations to support U.S. military action against terrorists. The military must enhance its capabilities and modify its policies to facilitate small-unit special forces operations, including covert operations, against terrorists. Congress must make clear that it will accept casualties in such operations.

AUGMENT HOMELAND SECURITY: Funds for reducing vulnerabilities and improving defenses in the United States should be significantly enhanced. Among the highest priorities should be the security of rail systems, chemical plants, and ports receiving shipping containers. Assistance to states and metropolitan areas should be based upon a requirements-driven, multiyear plan that provides each major metropolitan area with certain specific minimum essential capabilities.

PREVENT NUCLEAR TERRORISM: Although the probability of nuclear terrorism may not be high, the consequences of failure to prevent it would be catastrophic. The president should appoint a senior official to direct all U.S. nuclear nonproliferation and nuclear counterterrorism efforts. Such efforts should include new initiatives to provide international guarantees of nuclear energy supplies in exchange for agreement to terminate enrichment activities.

IMPROVE ENERGY SECURITY: Increasing U.S. dependence on Middle East oil is a failure of market forces and complicates our response to security issues in the region. The United States should, therefore, appropriate significant funds to subsidize a rapid shift to energy sources that do not rely upon oil and gas.

2. The Nature of the Threat

The Global War on Terrorism, as the Bush administration has labeled it, is actually a struggle by governments around the world to deal with a revivified radical and violent minority Islamist movement that has taken on greater international dimensions in the twenty-first century than it has previously in history. Throughout the twentieth century, radical groups arose in various Muslim nations seeking to use Islam as a justification for their use of violence against existing governments. These groups failed and seldom had a significant effect in more than one country at a time.

The Afghan War against the Soviets (1980–1988) served as a magnet for disenchanted elements from throughout the Islamic world. After that war, an informal network developed linking these violent radicals in over twenty nations. Subsequent struggles in Bosnia and Chechnya, in which Muslims fought non-Muslims, strengthened the network. By sharing their knowledge and experience, using the greatly expanded international travel and communications systems, these groups strengthened one another. They also shared funding, training, logistics, propaganda, and ideology. This sharing and the use of the new technologies transformed these groups into a global network dedicated to fighting "holy war" against those who do not share their views. Although the meaning of *jihad* in Islam is broader than fighting war, these radicals proclaim themselves as jihadists.

Goals at Home and in the West

In most predominately Muslim nations, the goal of these affiliated jihadist groups is to overthrow the existing government and replace it with a nondemocratic regime that would enforce a particular strain of fundamentalist Islam, suppressing individual freedoms and liberties. The theocracies they would create would resemble the suppressive government inflicted on most of Afghanistan during the reign of the Taliban. Some in the movement advocate a multinational theocratic government named a "caliphate," after earlier Islamic institutions. (The most radical avow their intention to create a global caliphate, forcing non-Muslims to convert to Islam.)

These jihadist groups view most Western governments, most notably the United States, as a barrier to the creation of the caliphates. They see Western governments as supportive of the existing systems in such countries as Algeria, Egypt, Saudi Arabia, Pakistan, Uzbekistan, and Indonesia. The jihadists also seek to expel non-Muslims and non-Muslim influences from Islamic countries. Thus, they oppose manifestations of globalism, such as the presence of European or American corporations.

In nations in which Muslims are the minority, such as in most of Europe and in the Americas, the jihadists seek to create subcultures that are insulated from the nations and societies in which they exist. They advocate "Islamic rights" and seek to strengthen Muslim institutions. Often they also use their presence in these nations as a base for propaganda, recruitment, fund-raising, and terrorism aimed at influencing the governments.

The Role of Nationalism

Often in the twentieth century, jihadists were involved in nationalist movements and struggles against colonialism. They were usually unsuccessful in affecting the subsequently created national governments. The international jihadist movement is now strengthened by the propaganda value of two ongoing nationalist struggles, in Palestine and in Iraq.

Although the current international jihadist movement has done little to assist the Palestinians, they have used the struggle of their fellow Muslims against Israel as a propaganda centerpiece for recruitment and fund-raising. There has also been some limited exchange of information and other relations between both the secular and "religious" Palestinian resistance groups and some in the international jihadist movement. Were the Palestinians and the government of Israel to reach and implement a comprehensive agreement such as the 2000 Camp David and Taba proposals, it would have little effect on the international jihadists, although it might somewhat diminish their support in parts of the Muslim world over time.

Although the U.S. invasion of Iraq was generally opposed in the Islamic world, many understood the heinous nature of the Saddam regime and welcomed its end. The ongoing U.S. military presence in Iraq, however, has widely been seen throughout the Islamic world as an unjustified military occupation akin to the Israeli military occupation of the West Bank and Gaza. The terrorist movements (both indigenous and foreign) involved in resisting the U.S. military presence have links to the international jihadist movement. Moreover, the movement successfully uses the U.S. occupation as a propaganda tool to recruit adherents and funds.

The fighting in Chechnya against the Russian government is also used for propaganda as an example of non-Muslim military occupation of an Islamic country.

Targeting the West to Affect the Islamic World

The jihadist movement uses terrorist attacks on the West, particularly the United States, for a variety of purposes:

- to influence American and Western opinion to demand abandonment of the U.S./Western presence in Islamic nations and the U.S./Western support of existing Islamic governments.

- to demonstrate to fellow Muslims that the United States and Western nations are not omnipotent and can be humbled by aggressive jihadist activity.

- to raise financial donations and new recruits by demonstrating "results" by their jihadist groups.

- to influence possible adherents in Islamic nations to join them in changing existing governments in those nations, by showing through the success of their attacks that the tide of history is on the side of the jihadists.

To achieve these purposes, the jihadists seek to conduct spectacular attacks, often involving iconic targets or targets that will affect key parts of a nation's economy (e.g., tourism, aviation, oil). The purpose of choosing these targets is to cause the population of the nation attacked to be either sufficiently shocked or put in sufficient economic pain to change its nation's policies vis-à-vis the Islamic world. The jihadists analyze the target nations' systems in detail, looking for vulnerabilities and weaknesses, looking for opportunities to create shock and financial cost.

There is an important question about the motivation of the jihadists: Some believe that they are motivated chiefly by U.S. actions with which they disagree, such as the invasion of Iraq or U.S. support of Israel. Others believe that the jihadists are primarily motivated by something they want to create, their concept of theocratic governments, rather than stopping something that the United States has done.

It is clear that the jihadists successfully employ criticism of U.S. activity as a way of widening their support (join the jihad if you oppose the United States in Iraq). That added support is a major factor in the continued growth in the jihadists' capabilities and threat. Whether or not the United States were in Iraq or Israel in the West Bank, however, the core jihadists would still seek to overthrow existing regimes to create theocracies. They would still target the United States because they believe American support of existing Islamic governments (the al Saud in Saudi Arabia, the Mubarak government in Egypt) makes their goal of replacing those governments harder to achieve.

AL QAEDA AND MORE—MUCH MORE

The group "al Qaeda" was founded in the late 1980s by one of the leaders in the international jihad movement, Osama bin Laden. Although al Qaeda was probably limited to a formal membership only in the hundreds at any one time, it also supported a larger cadre of jihadists in the several thousands. What al Qaeda did uniquely, however, was to assist other jihadist groups with organizational support, training, and financing:

- In nations where there were preexisting jihadist organizations, it provided the missing elements needed to strengthen them (Uzbekistan).

- In nations where there were no effective jihadist groups, it helped to create them (the Philippines).

- Freelance terrorists, such as Khalid Shaikh Muhammad, were able to gain logistical and financial support from al Qaeda and eventually merge their networks into the loose command structure of the organization.

- When the Egyptian Islamic Jihad (EIJ) organization was collapsing under effective counterterrorism efforts by the Cairo government, al Qaeda also permitted the EIJ to formally merge with it and made the EIJ leader, Ayman al-Zawahri, the nominal deputy in al Qaeda.

- To secure a nation-state sanctuary, al Qaeda provided funding and fighters (both its own and those from other jihadist groups) to support the Taliban regime in Afghanistan in its struggles against regional militias.

Thus, al Qaeda was primus inter pares among the jihadist groups. With the U.S. invasion of Afghanistan in 2001, al Qaeda lost its nation-state sanctuary (as it had earlier when ejected from Sudan in 1996). The U.S. invasion, while effective in driving the Taliban from power in most of Afghanistan, was less successful in destroying its primary target, al Qaeda. Significant U.S. ground forces were not introduced into the al Qaeda base areas until seven weeks into the invasion. The United States then chose to use its newfound Afghan allies to pursue the al Qaeda leadership into the Afghan-Pakistan border area, with limited success. (U.S. leaders defended their limited use of forces against the largely Arab al Qaeda paramilitary by citing the difficulties that the Soviet Red Army had encountered twenty years earlier in attempting to defeat Afghan forces. The two situations were not analogous.)

Al Qaeda after the Afghan Intervention

The result of this limited early use of U.S. forces in Afghanistan in 2001 was that most of the al Qaeda leadership and much of its paramilitary were able to escape immediate capture or death. (There were also reports that Pakistani Air Force flights into Afghanistan during the U.S. invasion assisted in the escape of some al Qaeda elements, or at least al Qaeda–related anti-Indian terrorists along with sympathetic Pakistani military advisers and military intelligence officers.)

Many al Qaeda personnel went to Pakistan, some staying in the mountainous border regions with Afghanistan, and others moving into the metropolitan areas of Karachi and Rawalpindi. Pakistani authorities, in cooperation with U.S. intelligence, subsequently arrested many key figures of al Qaeda (Khalid Shaikh Muhammad, Ramzi bin Al Sheeb) in Pakistani cities in 2002–2004. They have been less successful in finding al Qaeda leaders in the mountainous border areas, where both Osama bin Laden and his deputy, Ayman al-Zawahri, are widely believed to be. They have also had limited success in suppressing remnants of the Taliban, who are also believed to be engaged in transborder operations. (Taliban leader Mullah Omar is also still at large.)

Other al Qaeda leaders fled into Iran, elements of whose government had regularly supported and facilitated the travel of al Qaeda personnel throughout the late 1990s. The Tehran government claims that the al Qaeda personnel who entered the country have either been handed over to authorities in their home countries or are under "house arrest" in Iran. There is, however, some evidence that while in Iran, al Qaeda leaders sanctioned or directed terrorist attacks in Saudi Arabia.

"Two-Thirds of the Managers"

Based on the arrests in Afghanistan and Pakistan, U.S. authorities have repeatedly claimed that "two-thirds of the known al Qaeda managers have been captured or killed." These statements refer to the current status of the individuals who were believed to be members of al Qaeda's consultative council, or Shura, in the summer of 2001. The statements appear to be accurate, but they omit two important related elements:

- The two top leaders of al Qaeda remain at large now more than three years following the 9/11 attacks.

- Al Qaeda replaces "managers" when they are no longer able to carry out their responsibilities.

The success in eliminating al Qaeda leadership led many terrorism analysts to believe in 2003–2004 that al Qaeda as a terrorist organization was largely out of business. They portrayed the organization as left with only a few aged and sick former leaders, holed up in caves, cut off from the world, and unable to communicate except by occasionally smuggling out audiotapes on long mule rides to Arab media, such as al-Jazeera television reporters.

Following arrests in late summer 2004 in Pakistan and England, some analysts modified their views and suggested that the core al Qaeda organization does still exist as an organization, with a communications network of some sort linking its leaders with cells in Europe and elsewhere. If so, it is an organization with less experienced personnel, who may have greater difficulty communicating and conducting operations than they did prior to the elimination of the Afghan sanctuary. Nonetheless, the arrests in 2004 suggest that it is an organization still capable of planning large-scale terrorist attacks, recruiting personnel to carry them out, and obtaining explosives and other necessary logistics.

Al Qaeda always was, however, a relatively small terrorist group, with an inner core of several hundred and a cadre in the few thousands. Its strength lay in the network it had fostered with other jihadist groups. Whatever the truth is about the strength of al Qaeda today, the network is clearly still vibrant and dangerous.

THE THREAT OF THE HYDRA

With the exception of Chechen, and perhaps some Algerian, terrorist groups, few of the organizations in the jihadist network conducted large and successful terrorist attacks or campaigns prior to 9/11, except al Qaeda. (It was al Qaeda that staged the terrorist attacks in East Africa in 1998 and the attack on the USS *Cole* in Yemen in 2000. Several failed terrorist attacks in 1996–2000 were also attributable to al Qaeda. Personnel who later became key to al Qaeda were involved in the 1993 attack on the World Trade Center. Some analysts also believe that al

Qaeda may have assisted Iranian intelligence in the 1996 attack on the U.S. Air Force facility in Saudi Arabia.)

Following 9/11 and the disruption of al Qaeda, affiliated jihadist groups stepped up their attacks. In the three years following 9/11, these groups successfully carried out twice as many major attacks as they and al Qaeda had in the three years prior to 9/11. Whether this wave of terrorism was part of a preplanned al Qaeda response to a U.S. invasion of Afghanistan or was improvised by al Qaeda or the network, the result was a demonstration that with or without al Qaeda as a terrorist organization, the global jihadist network is still a threat. The connections among the various national groups already existed, thanks to al Qaeda, and are now strengthening.

Were Osama bin Laden to be captured or killed, both al Qaeda and the global jihadist network of which it is a part (although perhaps no longer primus inter pares) will continue to operate. Bin Laden is likely to become in death what he had already largely become after 9/11, a symbol that successful jihad can be waged against the United States and its friends.

THE CONCENTRIC CIRCLES OF JIHADISM

In thinking about the nature of the jihadist threat, it may be helpful to think of the relationship among distinct groups as four concentric circles (see Figure 2.1):

- In the smallest, inner circle are the terrorists of the al Qaeda organization, those who have been allowed the "privilege" of pledging their loyalty to the group and its leader. The population of this inner circle is probably in the hundreds.

- The second circle contains active members and devotees of another dozen or more jihadist groups that are often called "al Qaeda–related." (Those groups are examined in detail in Chapter 3.) Many, but probably not most, of these individuals are willing to commit terrorist acts personally, and some are willing to die in the process as suicide bombers. This second circle probably contains several tens of thousands of people.

- The third circle consists of those who identify with the jihadist cause or aspects of its ideology. They may provide moral support, and if called upon, some might facilitate logistical or financial activity in support of a jihadist group. This larger circle includes many who want to see their current government replaced by a different regime that might be less corrupt, more democratic, or more "Islamist." Among those who want new governments, there is a wide diversity of opinion regarding the model they seek; more democratic may not mean more "Islamist," and vice versa. This circle may be populated by tens of millions or perhaps as many as a few hundred million, depending upon the criteria (agreement in ideology versus willingness to assist a jihadist group) and the questions asked in polling data.

- The outer circle is that of the Islamic world, the followers of the Prophet Muhammad both in majority Islamic countries and scattered throughout the world. They number over 1 billion people. Most Muslims are not Arabs. They include 196 million in Indonesia, the nation with the largest Islamic population, 134 million in India, 133 million in China, 130 million in Pakistan and Bangladesh, 65 million in Iran, and 62 million in Turkey. Islam is also the fastest growing religion in the United States and Europe. An extremely small number (tenths of 1 percent) of Muslims are jihadists, although a growing number may be sympathetic to one or more aspects of the jihadist agenda such as the establishment of new governments.

Figure 2.1
The Concentric Circles of Jihadism

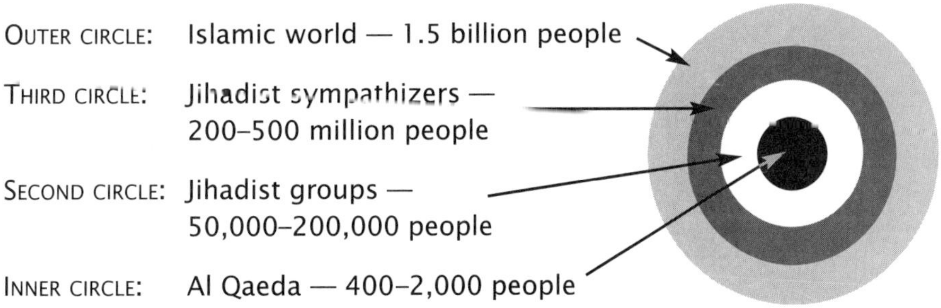

If the criteria for jihadist support were the belief that the U.S. military should depart Iraq or the Israeli military should depart the West Bank and Gaza, the majority of Muslims would probably agree. That agreement does not, however, translate into a willingness to support actively jihadist groups except among a small minority.

TARGETING THE RIGHT CIRCLES WITH THE RIGHT STRATEGIES

For the United States and the West in general, the responses we develop to the jihadist movement must distinguish among the components of the problem. To deal effectively with the threat, we must have consensus about the nature of the problem facing us. There should be clarity that the threat is not "terrorism," or even all terrorist organizations, but rather the jihadist terrorists who seek to hijack Islam and use violence to replace existing governments with nondemocratic theocracies.

The strategy and tactics that we employ to go after the two inner circles involve chiefly law enforcement and intelligence activities, sometimes supported by military measures. (Chapter 6 discusses how to improve these U.S. capabilities.) In addition, the United States must continue to provide intelligence, military, and financial support to other nations that are targeted by these jihadist groups:

- Within the two inner circles, the United States must give priority to al Qaeda itself, because al Qaeda has focused on the United States as a target more than any other jihadist group has.

- Priority among the other jihadist groups should be determined based upon their demonstrated capability and willingness to operate in the United States. Additional priority should be given to those groups that have targeted American facilities overseas (such as Jemaah Islamiyah's attack on the Marriott Hotel in Jakarta). For the other jihadist groups, U.S. activities should largely be in support of friendly governments that are the most likely potential targets of these jihadists. That U.S. assistance may be directly focused on the terrorist groups or more broadly on strengthening the friendly government, such as through trade policies or loans from international financial institutions.

The strategy and tactics that the United States must pursue to affect the third and fourth of the concentric circles go beyond law enforcement and intelligence measures and instead involve policies, values, and our ability to articulate and propagate those values. Here too, U.S. assistance to friendly governments is an important tool, particularly when that assistance is either (a) conditioned upon the friendly government ceasing to do things that create jihadist support (such as indiscriminate police crackdowns and widespread use of torture) or (b) aimed at enabling the friendly government to provide services that gain them increased support vis-à-vis the jihadists (such as offering better schools than the jihadists' so-called madrassas, which teach hatred as the major subject of the curriculum).

In addition to assistance, however, the United States must successfully promote discussion of shared values, including democracy, civil liberties, nonviolence, and protection of noncombatants. Traditional propaganda mechanisms, even updated to include satellite television, are a small part of the solution. U.S. activities in Iraq, as portrayed by many Islamic news media, make it difficult for the U.S. government to successfully promote these values and ideas in the Muslim world. Much of that task will have to be borne by nongovernmental organizations, governments other than the United States, and through leaders in the Islamic world. The U.S. government could, however, play a role in stimulating such groups, governments, and individuals to assume these tasks. (The Battle of Ideas is discussed in Chapter 5).

Key to the overall management of the U.S. response to the jihadist threat is an understanding of how U.S. actions affecting one of these four concentric circles impacts the other circles. It may well be, for example, that to defeat a jihadist terrorist group (second circle), the United States might choose to support a government that is widely disliked by its people for its corruption and suppression of civil liberties and democracy (such as Uzbekistan). Doing so, however, may be counterproductive to attempting to gain support in the third and fourth circles within that country. Understanding those trade-offs and making them explicitly and consciously will be key to the overall long-term success in suppressing the jihadists. In general, the long-term interests of the United States will be best served by actively influencing such governments to eliminate the causes of popular unrest, particularly when they involve civil liberties infringements and human rights abuses.

3. The Hydra of Jihad

To devise plans to counter the jihadist terrorist threat, we must understand in some detail its various manifestations, which vary by region. In this chapter, we examine twelve jihadist terrorist groups and four radicalizing organizations—that is, apparently nonviolent groups that advocate the same goals as the terrorists. Specialists will argue that other groups are equally worthy of inclusion. This analysis is not meant to exhaustively include the entire, ever-changing landscape of jihadists but rather is intended to detail most of the major groupings and to provide a general understanding of the jihadist hydra and its regional manifestations.

Southeast Asia

Abu Sayyaf Group (ASG)

Group Leader(s): Khadaffy Janjalani is the nominal leader of the Abu Sayyaf Group (Bearer of the Sword) and younger brother of the group's late founder, Abdurajak Janjalani. Abu Soliaman is a senior officer and group spokesman. Other key leaders include Isnilon Hapilon (operations chief), Radulan Sahiron (military commander), and Dr. Abu Pula (commander and paramedical expert). Senior leader Binang Andang was captured on August 1, 2004.

Current Size: ASG has a core of several hundred fighters, but the group is highly fragmented, so estimates of size vary. Before concentrated Philippine military action against the group started in 2000 following a spate of high-profile kidnappings, the group was thought to have as many as 4,000 members. Although the U.S.-backed campaign against

ASG significantly reduced its numbers, a sizable income from kidnap ransom probably allows the group to currently support somewhat fewer than 1,000 fighters, excluding a larger noncombatant support network. Some Philippine authorities argue that the group has as few as 300 fighters.

HISTORY: Abdurajak Janjalani founded ASG in 1991, splitting from its forerunner, the Moro National Liberation Front. Janjalani was an ex-mujahideen fighter in the Afghan-Soviet war, and his quest to establish an Islamic state in Southeast Asia began with a bloody campaign in the southern Philippines. ASG used kidnappings, bombs, and grenade attacks on Christian targets and foreigners to advance its objectives, conducting over 100 terrorist incidents in its first four years. For its series of attacks, ASG was listed by the U.S. State Department as a foreign terrorist organization in October 1997. As members of the criminal networks in the Philippines secured leadership positions in the group, a profit-driven kidnapping strategy began to eclipse ASG's Islamic ideology. This trend increased following Janjalani's death in late 1998, as the group fragmented into a quasi-confederation made up of primarily five bandit subgroups. In April 2000, ASG elements kidnapped twenty-one people, including ten Westerners, from two resorts in Malaysia. During the rest of 2000, a French film crew, twelve Christian Evangelists, and more than a dozen Filipinos were also taken hostage. Although some were rescued and a few released, the ASG reportedly earned millions in ransom payments, including a large amount from Libya in exchange for the remaining Westerners taken from the Malaysian resorts. American Jeffrey Schilling was also taken by an ASG subgroup in August but escaped from his captors in April 2001. In May 2001, another large group of people, including three Americans, was kidnapped from a resort in the southern Philippines. American Guillermo Sobero was executed in June, and several Filipino Christians were beheaded as well over the course of the year. American Martin Burnham was killed, and his wife injured, during a Philippine army rescue attempt in June 2002.

LINKS TO AL QAEDA: Al Qaeda's links to ASG are very strong. Under Abdurajak Janjalani's leadership, the group likely received regular financial support from Osama bin Laden during the 1990s. A number of its fighters likely trained in Afghanistan, including twenty group leaders who allegedly trained at an al Qaeda camp near Mazar-e-Sharif in northern Afghanistan in 2001. Janjalani also had strong ties to bin Laden's brother-in-law Mohammed Jamal Khalifa, who lived in the Philippines until 1996 and whose financial outlays for Islamic charities in Mindanao provided training and funds for ASG. Al Qaeda members Khalid Shaikh Muhammad and Ramzi Yousef worked on the Bojinka Plot to bomb U.S. airliners and assassinate the pope in late 1994 and early 1995 but do not appear to have had ASG assistance in their planning. Both extremists took scuba diving lessons in the southern Philippines during that period, however, and the trips may have been cover for the training of ASG members. Intelligence officials contend that two al Qaeda members were inside an ASG base on Basilan Island in the Philippines on the day after the 9/11 attacks.

ACTIVITIES AND ATTACKS SINCE 9/11: Since 9/11, ASG has been involved in hundreds of kidnappings, largely victimizing the local populations of the southern Philippines. In August 2002, the group kidnapped six Filipino Jehovah's Witnesses and beheaded two of them. In October 2002, the group bombed a restaurant across from a Philippine military base, killing three Filipinos and one U.S. serviceman. In February 2004, the group claimed responsibility for an explosion on a passenger ferry near the Philippine capital of Manila, which killed 130 passengers. ASG group leader Galib Andang (also known as Commander Robot), who was responsible for many of the kidnappings and beheadings of the prior years, was captured in Sulu in December 2003. Police arrested six members of ASG in March 2004 who were plotting bomb attacks on shopping malls, trains, Western embassies, and other targets in Manila. In June 2004, during the country's Independence Day celebration, one policeman was killed and two were wounded while trying to disarm a bomb placed by ASG operatives in the Plaza Rizal shopping center in Sulu Province in the southern Philippines.

OUTLOOK AND FUTURE INDICATORS FOR THE GROUP: The loose cell structure, inhospitable terrain, and wide support network in Sulu and Basilan provinces will continue to make it difficult for Filipino forces to eliminate the ASG. The various ASG elements will likely continue to operate in subgroups, focusing on Christian and Western targets of opportunity in the southern Philippines. The group will also likely try to stage more attacks in the metro Manila area in order to terrorize the populace and to try to undermine President Gloria Macapagal-Arroyo's administration.

ASG also seems to have made a few tactical shifts in recent months. First, recent attacks suggest the group may be developing an increased capacity for attacks on soft targets outside of the Mindanao and Sulu areas. Second, Filipino officials claim that ASG has made significant links to the deadliest Southeast Asian terrorist group, Jemaah Islamiya (JI). Officials argue that ASG has provided sanctuary for JI operatives in return for training. Third, there is evidence that the group's leader, Khadaffy Janjalani, is attempting to renew the group's focus on establishing an Islamic state in the southern Philippines. These three trends suggest that ASG has become, and will continue to be, increasingly receptive to the agendas, tactics, and ideologies of al Qaeda and other regional terrorist groups.

JEMAAH ISLAMIYA (JI)

GROUP LEADER(S): The two most prominent current JI leaders in Indonesia are Azahari Husin, a senior planner and explosives expert, and his associate Noordin Mohammad Top. Other key leaders include Nuim, alias Zuhroni (a veteran of the Afghan mujahideen and a major recruiter for the Ambon and Maluku conflicts), Abdul Rahim Ayub (alleged leader of JI's Australia operations), Zulkarnaen (the head of JI military operations and a member of the JI central command), and Dulmatin (an explosives expert). A key leader known as Mustaqim was arrested in August 2004. Abu Bakar Ba'asyir, JI's spiritual leader, has been in jail since October 2002 on charges of planning to assassinate current Indonesian president Megawati Sukarnoputri and for his involvement in a series of church bombings in 2000 in Indonesia and the Philippines.

CURRENT SIZE: JI has experienced several major setbacks in the last few years, including the capture of its operational chief, Nurjaman Riduan Ismuddin (also known as Hambali), in Thailand in August 2003. Currently, 200 men with alleged links to JI are in custody in Indonesia, Malaysia, Singapore, and the Philippines. But JI is believed to have grown to at least several thousand members and remains a threat. In addition, JI has cultivated links to local separatist and militant Islamic groups in Southeast Asia, including the Moro Islamic Liberation Front (MILF) and ASG.

HISTORY: JI was formally established on January 1, 1993. Most of its senior leadership had previously trained in Afghanistan in the late 1980s and early 1990s in the camps of the Saudi-financed Afghan mujahideen leader Abdul Rasul Sayyaf. JI adopted the goal of creating an Islamic state in Southeast Asia by 2025 comprising Brunei, Indonesia, Malaysia, Singapore, the southern Philippines, and southern Thailand. The JI network has thrived on ideological indoctrination, which is conducted at terror training camps throughout Southeast Asia and at a collection of Muslim boarding schools, known as pesantren, where young students are taught jihadist principles. JI has a loosely organized cell structure that is heavily dependent on a complicated web of marriage alliances that makes JI seem like one large extended family. Riduan Ismuddin, a.k.a. Hambali, a former senior attack planner, was widely regarded as JI's operational chief and played a key leadership role in the organization until his capture in August 2003. He was closely involved in many terrorist plots, headed JI's regional policymaking body, and is suspected of also being head of al Qaeda's operations for East Asia. Hambali was likely involved in one of the group's first international attacks, an August 2000 car bomb attack on the Jakarta home of the Philippine ambassador to Indonesia, in which the ambassador was wounded and two others were killed.

LINKS TO AL QAEDA: JI has numerous and well-documented ties to al Qaeda. Some U.S. officials and terrorism experts believe that JI is a subdivision of al Qaeda. Other experts believe that the JI network is not subservient to al Qaeda but rather cooperates with bin Laden's organization when it is mutually beneficial. JI has received funding and logistical assistance from al Qaeda. A Yemeni operative named Syafullah allegedly surfaced in Bali a few days before the October 2002 bombings and then left the night of the bombings. In return, JI has cased targets and assisted al Qaeda members' travels through Southeast Asia. Prominently, Hambali arranged a meeting between two of the 9/11 hijackers and key al Qaeda figures in Malaysia in January 2000. Hambali also arranged for a group of JI teenagers, including Hambali's younger brother, to study at religious madrassas in Karachi, Pakistan, prior to the 9/11 attacks. The "al-Ghuraba" cell members allegedly received training in weapons and explosives training in Afghanistan, and some met with bin Laden. The cell was disrupted in September 2003, and all of the members were deported back to Malaysia and Indonesia. Five were charged with having trained to carry out attacks on behalf of al Qaeda against American interests in Malaysia, though no specific targets were specified.

ACTIVITIES AND ATTACKS SINCE 9/11: U.S. officials maintain that Hambali was helping to develop an al Qaeda chemical and biological weapons program before it was disrupted by the invasion of Afghanistan following the 9/11 attacks. There is evidence that JI and al Qaeda planners were preparing to coordinate a 9/11 "second strike" on U.S. West Coast targets with planes hijacked in Southeast Asia. In December 2001, authorities in Singapore discovered a JI plot to attack U.S., Israeli, British, and Australian diplomatic targets in Singapore. In October 2002, JI executed the Bali nightclub blasts, which killed 202. The blasts targeted Western tourists and used an electronic trigger to detonate a 300-pound ammonium nitrate fertilizer car bomb. That same month, JI was designated a foreign terrorist organization by the United States. JI operatives were also involved in bombings at Davao International Airport and Davao Wharf, both in the Philippines, in the spring of 2003. In June, another JI plot to attack several Western embassies and tourist sites in Singapore was disrupted. The August J.W. Marriott Hotel bombing in Jakarta, which killed twelve, targeted Americans and U.S. government officials and used a suicide car bomb. In October 2003, Filipino police raided a JI safe house in the Philippines and found bomb-making materials and manuals in Indonesian describing how to make biological and chemical weapons. Traces of biological weapons were also allegedly found in the apartment. In June 2004, it was reported that JI had sent a special terrorist cell into Indonesia to assassinate diplomats from Australia and other Western countries.

OUTLOOK AND FUTURE INDICATORS FOR THE GROUP: Although JI has recently weathered numerous setbacks, such as the capture of some of its most influential leaders, the so-called second generation of JI leaders is innovating and could develop an even more effective organization than previously existed. The "second generation" of JI leaders appears to be even more dedicated to jihad than its predecessors. Many of these new leaders are the children of JI members. Indoctrinated with JI's mission and tactics from their youth, they were able to train in Indonesian religious clashes in the Ambon and Poso regions and have vowed to spawn new terrorist cells to continue their holy war. There is some evidence that this second generation of JI leaders may be even more sympathetic to bin Laden's call to adopt increasing violent tactics against Western targets. At the same time, there is evidence that a rift within JI is emerging with regard to how and when the group should wage its jihad. Most disturbingly, JI seems bent on developing chemical and biological weapons capabilities, and the recently discovered chem-bio manual in the Philippines is an indicator that the group continues to explore their development.

MIDDLE EAST—AFRICA

AL-ITTIHAD AL-ISLAMI (AIAI)

GROUP LEADER(S): Hassan Abdullah Hersi al-Turki is a key Somalia-based AIAI faction leader and supporter of al Qaeda. The U.S. secretary of state has placed al-Turki on the U.S. terrorist list, claiming he is "associated with al Qaeda and has provided support for acts of terrorism." Somaliland sources have identified Mohamed Ali as the group's leader for the Togdheer region in central Somaliland.

CURRENT SIZE: U.S. intelligence agencies estimate that AIAI has around 2,000 members, though only a portion of the group is considered actively militant. After incurring heavy losses in battles with the Ethiopian military, the group now operates mostly in small cells.

HISTORY: AIAI emerged in Somalia in the early 1990s after the regime of Siad Barre collapsed in 1991. As factions fought for territory, AIAI carved a spot for itself in the Gedo region, where the borders of Somalia, Kenya, and Ethiopia converge. AIAI hoped to turn Somalia into a fundamentalist Islamic state, and to achieve this goal the group began establishing regional Islamic schools and aid agencies. To avoid being targeted, AIAI integrated itself into the local communities and quickly won local support as it delivered relief services to the poorest communities. AIAI's regional ambitions grew, and it adopted the goal of creating a fundamentalist Islamic state in the Horn of Africa, though it continued to conduct the majority of its attacks against Ethiopia. AIAI is believed to be responsible for numerous bomb attacks on soft targets in the Ethiopian capital, Addis Ababa, between 1996 and 1997. In June 1998, the group kidnapped six International Red Cross members in Ethiopia, releasing them unharmed a month later. In April 2000, AIAI attacked and killed twelve Ethiopian soldiers. AIAI has mostly operated in small units using guerrilla warfare tactics and explosives' expertise to inflict maximum damage on their victims. AIAI has mainly operated in Somalia but maintains a limited presence in Kenya and Ethiopia. The group has not been designated as a foreign terrorist organization.

LINKS TO AL QAEDA: Although some Somalia experts, such as Ted Dagne of the Congressional Research Service, contend that AIAI's strength and links to international terrorists are exaggerated, several U.S. officials have argued that AIAI received weapons and funding from bin Laden in the late 1990s. Despite this, AIAI has not yet been designated a foreign terrorist organization. On March 11, 2002, the United States charged the Somalia branch of the Al Haramain Islamic Foundation with supporting terrorist activities, including support for both AIAI and al Qaeda. On March 19, 2004, attacks on aid workers in Somaliland led to the arrest of five men who admitted to being members of AIAI and a part of an al Qaeda cell. Although these events do not provide incontrovertible evidence of cooperation between the two groups, the data suggest that a cooperative arrangement between AIAI and al Qaeda is highly possible.

ACTIVITIES AND ATTACKS SINCE 9/11: Israeli and U.S. officials suspect that members of AIAI assisted an al Qaeda cell in carrying out a suicide car bomb attack on a hotel in Kenya in November 2002, which killed eleven Kenyans and three Israelis, and a simultaneous failed attempt to shoot down a chartered El Al airliner that was leaving Nairobi and carrying Israeli tourists. AIAI members are suspected to be the perpetrators of a grenade attack on an Ethio-Kenyan Hotel in May 2003. The group killed two British teachers in Somaliland in October 2003 and was almost certainly responsible for the March 2004 attack on a German Agency for Technical Assistance (GTZ) vehicle in Somaliland, in which a Kenyan and a Somali were killed and a German was wounded. AIAI has also continued to engage in firefights and bombings against Ethiopian forces in eastern Ethiopia.

OUTLOOK AND FUTURE INDICATORS FOR THE GROUP: An FBI counterterrorism report from March 2003 maintained that AIAI and al Qaeda members were receiving scuba diving training in Somalia in order to prepare for attacks on ships. If the report is accurate, then AIAI is probably trying to develop the capability to mount attacks on ships passing around the Horn of Africa. AIAI members will likely continue to provide support to remaining East Africa–based al Qaeda members, and the group will continue efforts to expand the amount of territory it controls. In general, AIAI is purported to be well organized and highly insular. Thus, counterterrorism officials in the region will continue to find it very difficult to infiltrate the organization.

ISLAMIC ARMY OF ADEN-ABYAN (IAA)

GROUP LEADER(S): Khalid Abdulnabi, the leader of IAA, was recently apprehended by Yemeni authorities and then pardoned by Yemen's president, Ali Abdullah Saleh, along with many other captured militants, who claimed they had reformed themselves. It remains unclear whether Abdulnabi will retain a central role in IAA leadership and operations. Another key figure is Abu Hamza al-Masri, the self-described media adviser to IAA. Abu Hamza resides in London where he was, until recently, preaching at the Finsbury Park Mosque. British authorities arrested him in May 2004, and both the U.S. and Yemeni governments have requested his extradition.

CURRENT SIZE: The current size of IAA in unknown.

HISTORY: The Sunni militant group emerged in 1998 when it issued a series of statements in support of Osama bin Laden, called for the overthrow of the Yemeni government, and encouraged operations against U.S. and other Western interests in Yemen. Led by Zein al-Abidin al-Mihdar (a.k.a. Abu al-Hassan) and operating primarily in Yemen's southern governates of Aden and Abyan, IAA has argued that Yemen's government is not implementing shari'a law properly. The group had ties with al Qaeda since its founding, providing safe haven in exchange for funding. In December 1998, the group abducted sixteen British, American, and Australian tourists in southern Yemen, four of whom were killed during a rescue attempt. On October 12, 2000, al Qaeda operatives successfully attacked the USS *Cole*, killing seventeen U.S. sailors, injuring thirty-nine, and causing over $250 million in damage. IAA issued a communiqué through Abu Hamza in the United Kingdom claiming responsibility, although bin Laden was later identified as having personally approved the attack. The day after the *Cole* attack, IAA attempted a Molotov cocktail attack on the British Embassy in Yemen's capital, Sanaa. The group has not been designated as a foreign terrorist organization.

LINKS TO AL QAEDA: A government crackdown on IAA in 1999 led to the execution of its chief, Abu Bakr al-Mehdar. Following the crackdown, IAA retreated to Hatat, Yemen, where the group incorporated al Qaeda members into its ranks. More recently, IAA provided vocal support for bin Laden's terrorist activities and may have provided logistical support for al Qaeda operations, including the failed attempt to bomb the USS *Sullivan* and the successful attack on the USS *Cole*. Although IAA is independent from al Qaeda, the group has clearly established significant ties to al Qaeda and has facilitated al Qaeda activities in Yemen in the past. Following some government successes against both groups, it is unknown how extensive current ties are.

ACTIVITIES AND ATTACKS SINCE 9/11: IAA has been very active since September 11 and has made numerous attempts on high-profile Western targets. A string of bombings in 2001 was attributed to IAA, with targets including an Anglican Church in Aden and the Yemen-Intercontinental Hotel. IAA members were captured in 2001 while plotting to bomb the U.S. Embassy in Sanaa. In October 2002, the group claimed responsibility for an al Qaeda suicide boat attack on the French oil tanker *Limburg*, killing one person, injuring several, and spilling oil into the Hadramawt waters off the coast of Yemen. The group likely did conduct a June 2003 attack on a medical assistance convoy in the Abyan Governate of Yemen.

OUTLOOK AND FUTURE INDICATORS FOR THE GROUP: Due to the general lawlessness, wide availability of weaponry, and tribal control of many Yemeni provinces, the country will continue to be vulnerable to al Qaeda and IAA operatives unless there are dramatic changes in Yemen's counterterrorism policies. Yemeni president Saleh has periodically ordered the release of jailed terror suspects, including members of IAA, who have been "reeducated" and have supposedly renounced terrorism.

IAA will most likely continue to attack high-profile Western targets, possibly preying on targets of opportunity in Yemen's ungoverned hinterlands, as well as in unprotected ports and bays along the Yemeni coast.

SALAFIST GROUP FOR PREACHING AND COMBAT (GSPC)

GROUP LEADER(S): The head of GSPC, Nabil Sahraoui, was killed by the Algerian Army in June 2004, and the two most likely successors are Yahya Jawadi, a member of al-Fath Battalion, which operates in Algeria's eastern and southeastern districts, and Abu-Ammar, leader of the group in the west. Amari Saifi (also known as General Abderrezak "the Para") is a senior leader of GSPC currently being held in detention by the Chadian rebel group the Movement for Democracy and Justice in Chad (MDJT). MDJT has agreed to turn Abderrezak over to Algerian authorities, but the group has not yet done so. Abu-Yasir Sayyaf is a prominent member of the GSPC's information council, and Tarek Maaroufi is a key figure in GSPC's recruiting and cell-coordinating operations in Europe. Maaroufi is wanted in Italy, but authorities are unable to extradite him because of his Belgian citizenship.

CURRENT SIZE: GSPC's strength is unknown, but estimates range from 300 to 700 members spread throughout Algeria and Europe.

HISTORY: With the help of bin Laden, GSPC grew out of the Armed Islamic Group (GIA), the largest terrorist group in Algeria in the early 1990s. In that decade, GIA and GSPC together were responsible for the deaths of over 100,000 Algerians. By 1998, GSPC had surpassed GIA as the most effective terrorist group in Algeria; by 2000, the group had taken over GIA's networks of operatives and funding across Europe and North Africa. Haydar Abu Doha (also known as "The Doctor") played a large role in GSPC's transformation from a local armed group to an international terrorist organization. Using its new links to Europe, GSPC recruited heavily among the large base of Algerian teenagers on the continent, with particular success in France. GSPC dedicated itself to toppling the Algerian government as well as to conducting operations against Western targets in North Africa. The depth of its network in Europe was apparent when Italian police discovered a cell in Milan in April 2000 and French police discovered a cell in France in 2000.

LINKS TO AL QAEDA: Bin Laden helped to establish GSPC in the late 1990s as an alternative to GIA. GSPC leader Doha served as a senior figure at one of al Qaeda's Afghan terrorist camps before moving to the United Kingdom in 1999. After GSPC assumed control of GIA's networks in Europe, the group began to leverage its European contacts to facilitate al Qaeda funding and recruiting on the continent. Some experts believe that GSPC worked closely with al Qaeda experts from Georgia's Pankisi Gorge to establish a "ricin network" throughout Europe. Partially in response to the group's increasing international links, the group was designated a foreign terrorist organization by the U.S. State Department in March 2002. When Nabil Sahraoui took over leadership of GSPC in September 2003, he declared the group's alliance to al Qaeda.

ACTIVITIES AND ATTACKS SINCE 9/11: On January 4, 2003, GSPC killed fifty-one Algerian security personnel, which is the greatest loss ever by the Algerian Army from a single guerrilla attack. In February 2003, GSPC kidnapped thirty-one European tourists in the Algerian desert and the German government paid the group 5 million Euros for their release. In June 2004, the GSPC "al-Borkane" cell attacked the Hamma Power Station near Algiers with a truck bomb, damaging Algeria's most important electricity production facility and injuring eleven.

OUTLOOK AND FUTURE INDICATORS FOR THE GROUP: GSPC has dispersed itself across the border regions of Algeria, Mali, Libya, Mauritania, Niger, and Chad, and will therefore be difficult to contain in North Africa and the Sahel. In July 2004, a GSPC camp was discovered in the mountains of Tibesti, which span Libya's southern border with Chad. GSPC has also established a sophisticated recruiting network across Europe, which makes prevention of the emergence of new cells in Europe very difficult. The Dutch Internal Security Agency reported recently that GSPC has been recruiting young Muslim immigrants at mosques in the Netherlands. Algerian GSPC member Mohammed Bouhmidi was recently arrested in France after training in Belgium to become a diver. French authorities suspected that he was planning a maritime terrorist attack.

Salafiya Jihadiya

Group Leader(s): Abdelkrim Mejati is a top leader in Salafiya Jihadiya and is reported to be one of the masterminds of the group's massive attacks in Casablanca in May 2003. Also serving as an operative for al Qaeda, Mejati is an explosives expert, is married to an American, and visited the United States during 2001. British-born Youssef El-Jamaiqui is also believed to be a key operative for Salafiya Jihadiya.

Current Size: Moroccan officials believe that 300 members of Salafiya Jihadiya attended al Qaeda camps in Afghanistan. The total group membership is most likely higher, given that the group recruits heavily in poor suburbs of several Moroccan cities.

History: Salafiya Jihadiya, created by former Afghan mujahideen, became active in the 1990s. The group was founded on Wahhabi principles, and the group's spiritual leader, Mohammad al-Fizazi, preached anti-Western messages in Tangiers before receiving a thirty-year prison sentence for inciting violence in Morocco. Some of its members have come from middle-class backgrounds, having become frustrated by their secondary status in Europe, but many have been recruited from slums in Morocco. Most of its core members have received training in al Qaeda's camps in Afghanistan. The group has not been designated as a foreign terrorist organization.

Links to al Qaeda: Salafiya Jihadiya has sent many members to train in Afghan terror camps and the group has also received some direction and funding from al Qaeda. In spite of its numerous links to al Qaeda, the planning and execution for its operations, including the bombings in Casablanca, are largely homegrown.

Activities and Attacks Since 9/11: In mid-May 2003, Salafiya Jihadiya launched coordinated suicide bombing attacks on multiple targets in Casablanca, including an old Jewish cemetery, a luxury hotel, the Belgian consulate, a Jewish-owned Italian restaurant, and a Spanish social club. The attacks killed forty-three and injured 100 people. One of the key planners of the attacks, Pierre Robert, converted to Islam in

1990 and is alleged to have links with al Qaeda. Robert is also alleged to have been planning more terrorist attacks in Europe, including an attack on a French nuclear power plant. In September 2003, Moroccan police disrupted a Salafiya Jihadiya cell in Rabat and arrested twenty-four group members. The group included two sisters who had agreed to attack soft targets, including a supermarket that had been selected eight months prior. Spanish investigators found that the Moroccan Islamic Combatant Group (GICM)—responsible for the infamous Madrid bombings, which killed almost 200 people in mid-March 2004—has connections to Salafiya Jihadiya. Sixteen of those arrested in Spain during investigations were said to be members of Al Oussououd Al Khalidine (The Eternal Lions), which is a Salafiya Jihadiya cell in Spain.

OUTLOOK AND FUTURE INDICATORS FOR THE GROUP: Salafiya Jihadiya may have incurred a major setback in the immediate aftermath of the Casablanca bombings, when Moroccan authorities purportedly arrested between 100 and 200 suspected members. The group has a deep roster, however, and as one Moroccan official put it, "You have to assume that if there were fifteen willing to blow themselves up, there are dozens more still waiting in line." The disruption of several more cells since the 2003 Casablanca attacks indicates that the group continues to actively recruit and plan for additional attacks.

IRAQ

JAMA'AT AL-TAWHID W'AL-JIHAD (JTJ)

GROUP LEADER(S): Abu Mus'ab al-Zarqawi leads JTJ. His subcommanders in JTJ are likely experienced Jordanians, Syrians, and possibly Iraqi Kurds he has worked with in the past. Zarqawi, who grew up in a Palestinian refugee camp in Jordan and went to Afghanistan in the late 1980s, developed ties to future al Qaeda members. After being imprisoned in Jordan in 1992–1999 for conspiring to overthrow the monarchy and establish an Islamic caliphate, he returned to Afghanistan and ran his own al Qaeda–linked training camp near Herat. Zarqawi is a follower of the extreme Takfiri ideology of Sunni Islam, in which all non-Muslims, as well as all Shia, are considered apostates who should be killed if they do not convert. Although Zarqawi has close ties to Osama bin Laden, he never swore the oath of Bayat (allegiance) to him and appears to be setting his own agenda with JTJ attacks on coalition, Iraqi government, and Shia targets. Zarqawi played an integral part in al Qaeda planning for attacks to take place in Jordan as part of the Millennium Plot in late 1999. The foiled plot would have targeted Westerners and Israelis at Western hotels in Amman, including the Radisson SAS. For his part in the plot, Zarqawi was convicted in absentia and sentenced to death.

Current Size: U.S. and coalition officials estimate that JTJ currently has between 400 and 1,000 members. The cell-based structure of the group and the fluid nature of alliances among foreign fighter groups in Iraq make it difficult to determine the group's strength.

History: The Jama'at al-Tawhid w'al-Jihad (Unity and Jihad Group), made up primarily of non-Iraqi Arabs, was created in Iraq probably during the late summer of 2003. Founder Abu Mus'ab al-Zarqawi has created a cell-based structure for the group, with independent cells operating in cities across central and northern Iraq, including Mosul, Baghdad, Fallujah, and Ramadi. JTJ's original goal in 2003 was to try to cause the U.S.-led coalition in Iraq to fail, while creating the conditions for the establishment of a fundamentalist Islamic government. With the late June 2004 transfer of power, JTJ's current goals are to try to destroy the new Iraqi Interim Government (IIG) through assassinations of key officials and attacks on government infrastructure. At the same time, JTJ is seeking to drive both allied countries and logistical contracting companies out of the coalition through attacks on coalition convoys and by taking hostages in order to force both away from the U.S.-led effort.

Links to al Qaeda: Despite Zarqawi's long history of close links to al Qaeda, he has developed his own independent network in Iraq, where al Qaeda has not yet been able to build a significant presence. Zarqawi met with al Qaeda facilitator Hasan Ghul in January and passed him a letter to be given to bin Laden that laid out his plans for Iraq. He indicated in the letter, which was found when Ghul was captured trying to leave Iraq, that his group would try to disrupt the coalition and try to foment a civil war in Iraq by attacking Shia targets to such a degree that they would begin attacking Iraqi Sunnis in response. Zarqawi asked for bin Laden's blessing, but he implied that bin Laden's consent was not necessary for him to continue his operations.

ACTIVITIES AND ATTACKS SINCE 9/11: After the fall of the Taliban, Zarqawi fled Afghanistan and made his way to the Middle East. He was in Baghdad in the spring of 2002 and organized a regional network to help develop and distribute toxins that were being developed at camps of Kurdish terrorist ally Ansar al-Islam (AI) in northeastern Iraq. Although the network appeared to have failed to produce a significant amount of toxins to be used in operations, Zarqawi had a wide network of contacts in Europe and the Caucasus with whom he was in contact during that period. In October 2002, while possibly based at an AI camp, Zarqawi directed the assassination of USAID officer Lawrence Foley in Jordan. At the beginning of Operation Iraqi Freedom, Ansar al-Islam's camps were destroyed and Zarqawi went into hiding until August 2003, when JTJ likely was formed. JTJ is able to draw on jihadist volunteers and donors from across the Middle East, and it has used a network of facilitators to move recruits and money into Iraq, most prominently via Syria and Iran.

In August, suicide car bombs exploded at the Jordanian Embassy in Baghdad and at the Shrine of the Imam Ali mosque in An Najaf, leaving eighty-two dead, including leading Shia cleric Ayatollah Mohammed Bakir al-Hakim. Also in August, a suicide truck bomb attacked the UN headquarters in Baghdad. The UN secretary-general's special envoy to Iraq, Sergio Vieira de Mello was killed along with twenty-four others, leading to the UN's withdrawal from Iraq. In September, a suicide car bomb was stopped at the entrance to UN headquarters in Baghdad, killing only the driver of the car. In October, Zarqawi's network carried out suicide car bomb attacks against the Baghdad Hotel, which was housing Westerners, as well as the International Committee of the Red Cross (ICRC) headquarters in Baghdad, killing thirty-five. In November, a suicide truck bomb attacked Italian military police headquarters in Nasariyah, killing twenty-nine.

Starting in October and continuing to the present day, suicide car bombs have targeted Iraqi police stations and recruiting centers as well as coalition targets. In March 2004, four suicide bombers attacked Shia pilgrims and worshipers in Baghdad and Karbala during the Shia holy festival of Ashura, leaving 143 dead and over 400 wounded. The Basra port oil facility was targeted in late April in JTJ's first naval attack. In May, a suicide car bomb killed Iraqi Governing Council president Ezzedine Salim. Also in May, U.S. contractor Nicholas Berg was executed, probably by Zarqawi himself, and the incident was used for media value. This led to a string of hostage takings and executions by JTJ and Iraqi insurgent groups, including the execution of South Korean Kim Sun-Il by JTJ in June. In mid-August, JTJ posted on the Internet the execution of Egyptian Mohammed Fawzi Abdaal Mutwalli, who the group alleged had been working for the coalition as a spy. JTJ has also used its propaganda Internet sites to post several death threats against IIG prime minister Ayad Allawi.

JTJ also attempted to carry out an attack against the government of Jordan, for which Zarqawi has a deep enmity. Arrests of JTJ operatives in March and April in several locations across Jordan revealed a plot to bomb the headquarters of Jordan's General Intelligence Directorate, using probably a large improvised chemical weapon. JTJ later released an audiotape, probably by Zarqawi, in which he confirmed the target of the foiled attack and said to expect more attacks in the region. Zarqawi now has a robust network in Iraq with multiple semi-autonomous cells able to pick the target and timing of attacks. JTJ's total manpower has probably increased in 2004 as a result of Zarqawi's rising international prominence, which has likely resulted in smaller foreign extremist and Iraqi groups merging with JTJ. These additions would supplement the group's influx of recruits entering Iraq from the Persian Gulf. JTJ has not yet been designated a foreign terrorist organization.

Outlook and Future Indicators: JTJ will likely continue to attack coalition and IIG targets for the foreseeable future. With the withdrawal of the U.S. military presence from Fallujah, JTJ now has a safe haven within Iraq from which it can operate freely. It appears that JTJ would continue to function in the short term if Zarqawi were captured or killed. However, the loss of his propaganda and leadership value could cause the group to fracture due to loss of support and internal struggles. Similarly, Iraqi insurgent groups may attempt to push JTJ, composed of foreigners, out of Iraq. For now, JTJ rivals al Qaeda as the most prominent terrorist group operating in the Middle East. Given Zarqawi's past experience developing toxins at al Qaeda camps in Afghanistan, recent indications that the group is attempting to produce crude toxins are cause for concern.

ANSAR AL-ISLAM (AI)

GROUP LEADER(S): Abu 'Abdallah al-Shafi'i currently leads Ansar al-Islam (Supporters of Islam). Prior group leader Najm Faraj Ahmad, a.k.a. Mullah Krekar, who has held refugee status in Norway since 1991, had served as a key propagandist and fund-raiser among Europe's minority Kurdish population during the 1990s. He was arrested in Iran in September 2002, and after being flown to the Netherlands and briefly detained, he returned to Norway. Krekar has been arrested several times for extremist comments calling for attacks in Iraq and against America but is currently out of jail and under surveillance. Hemin Benishari has been named as AI's expert in assassinations and military tactics. He escaped into Iran in the spring of 2003 and his current whereabouts are unknown. Aso Hawleri was third in command of the group until his arrest by coalition forces in Mosul in October 2003. Ayoub Afghani, AI's senior explosives expert, was captured in Baghdad in March 2004.

CURRENT SIZE: Prior to the start of the war in Iraq, AI may have had upward of 2,000 fighters, including a number of al Qaeda members. Following losses at the start of the war and a number of arrests, deaths, and desertions since, the group is believed to currently field between 500 and 1,000 Iraqi Kurdish fighters, with many operating in cells in cities across central and northern Iraq.

HISTORY: Ansar al-Islam formed in late 2001 in a merger between the Islamic Movement of Kurdistan (IMK), led by Mullah Krekar, and the al Qaeda–affiliated Kurdish group Jund al-Islam, led by Abu 'Abdallah al-Shafi'i. Originally based in northeastern Iraq and made up almost exclusively of Sunni Iraqi Kurds, the group's goals prior to the war in Iraq were to create a fundamentalist Islamic state in the autonomous Kurdish zone that existed during Saddam's rule. AI controlled about a dozen villages and has fought for additional territory with two rival secular Kurdish groups, the Patriotic Union of Kurdistan (PUK), and to a lesser extent, the Kurdistan Democratic Party (KDP). Mullah Krekar approved the use of AI camp facilities by al Qaeda and Zarqawi's network to work on toxins development in 2002 in exchange for al Qaeda funding. AI official Abu 'Abdallah al-Shafi'i took command of the group in late 2003 as AI was setting up cells to conduct operations against coalition forces in Iraq and it became apparent that Mullah Krekar was not going to return to Iraq.

LINKS TO AL QAEDA: Al Qaeda likely provided AI with a large amount of funding that allowed it to successfully operate from its enclave from 2001 to early 2003. Extremists who would later join AI trained in al Qaeda camps in Afghanistan in the 1990s, and al Qaeda was likely more than happy to help fund AI following the loss of its Afghan safe haven in 2001. Al Qaeda's toxins program was operational at two AI bases from early 2002 until March 2003, overseen by Zarqawi and his associates. From his AI safe haven, Zarqawi directed the activities of other elements of his regional network. In 2004, al Qaeda has come under increasing pressure, and JTJ is carrying out the majority of anti-coalition attacks in Iraq. With no significant attacks since February, AI appears to be struggling to remain a major player in Iraq. Similarly, it is unclear how strong current contact is between AI and al Qaeda.

ACTIVITIES AND ATTACKS SINCE 9/11: Throughout 2002, AI provided safe haven to a group of al Qaeda members while simultaneously conducting military operations against rival PUK forces. The group failed in an assassination attempt against PUK Kurdistan Regional Government prime minister Saleh in April 2002. Following the start of the war in Iraq, most of AI's infrastructure and military capabilities was destroyed in April by air strikes, and some members were killed or captured. A significant number escaped into Iran, where group leaders are rumored to have received aid from Iran's Islamic Revolutionary Guard Corps (IRGC). After reconstituting its strength, most of AI's forces have since returned to Iraq. AI's first attack after the war in Iraq was in late November, when a suicide car bomb attack on the headquarters of the KDP office in Kirkuk killed five people. AI conducted another suicide car bomb attack on the Kurdish Interior Ministry building in Irbil in late December, killing five and wounding 101. In AI's most destructive attack, two suicide bombers attacked a joint KDP and PUK party office during a political meeting in early February 2004, killing 109 and wounding 235. These attacks were listed prominently when AI was designated a foreign terrorist organization by the U.S. State Department in March 2004. Over the same time frame, AI has lost some prestige and possibly some membership to Zarqawi's JTJ as a result of the low number of attacks it has conducted. AI fighters have been identified operating in Fallujah and other central Iraqi cities in conjunction with JTJ.

OUTLOOK AND FUTURE INDICATORS: AI has become less effective than Zarqawi's JTJ through an apparent loss of resources and manpower and has conducted far fewer attacks over the past year. The group, in its current cell-based structure, will likely continue to conduct attacks on coalition forces and on KDP and PUK opponents in northern Iraq as well. With the very low probability that AI will be able to reestablish its northeastern Iraqi sanctuary as long as coalition forces remain in Iraq, AI's short-term goal, similar to JTJ, is to try to disrupt IIG and coalition efforts to unify Iraq. AI continues to hold very similar ideological and strategic goals as al Qaeda and may be able to tap into contacts in Europe's significant Kurdish population to establish cells and carry out attacks in Europe. It is also unclear how close group leaders remain to radical elements in Iran. If the links are significant, Iranian elements may try to use AI as a proxy force to conduct attacks against coalition forces in Iraq if necessary. The same radical elements could use AI to try to conduct attacks inside the United States if Iran becomes actively engaged in the war on terror.

ASBAT AL-ANSAR

GROUP LEADER(S): Asbat al-Ansar (League of the Followers) was founded by Shaykh Hicham el-Shreidi, a fighter in the Lebanese civil war in the 1980s. In 1991, Shreidi was assassinated on the orders of Amin Kayid, the commander of Yasser Arafat's Fatah movement in the Ayn al-Hilwah refugee camp. Abu Muhjin has replaced him as the group's leader and has been responsible for shaping the group's current agenda. He has been sentenced to death in absentia in Lebanon for his role in the 1994 assassination of Sheikh Nizar al-Halabi, the leader of Al Ashbashi (The Ethiopian Organization). Despite this, Abu Muhjin remains at large and has directed assassinations against members of rival Palestinian groups operating in the Ayn al-Hilwah refugee camp, including members of Yasir Arafat's Fatah movement.

CURRENT SIZE: The group has approximately 300 members. Membership is almost entirely made up of Palestinians, and most of its members are based inside the Ayn al-Hilwah refugee camp in southern Lebanon.

HISTORY: Formed in 1985 as a faction in the Lebanese civil war, the radical Sunni group is made up primarily of Palestinians and advocates Salafism, a return to the ancient caliphate system of government. Asbat al-Ansar has had two political goals since its creation: the establishment of a fundamentalist Islamic state in Lebanon, and the prevention of any lasting peace between the Arab states and Israel. Despite this, Asbat al-Ansar has had a mostly ineffectual history of attacks. Attacks since the 1990s have involved low-level bombings of "un-Islamic" targets such as casinos and churches. Asbat al-Ansar has also targeted secular Palestinian groups in the Ayn al-Hilwah camp to increase its own influence. The group was responsible for an explosion at Lebanon's Customs Department and a 1999 attack on a Sidon, Lebanon, courthouse in which four judges were killed. In Asbat al-Ansar's first attack on a non-Arab target and its most significant attack to date, a rocket-propelled grenade attack by member Abu Kharab against the Russian Embassy in Beirut in January 2000 resulted in his death and eight Lebanese police casualties. The next week, Lebanese police disrupted an attempt by four suspected members of the group, disguised as soldiers, to launch another attack on the Russian Embassy. Asbat al-Ansar members participated in the jihads in Chechnya, Kashmir, Bosnia, and Afghanistan during the 1990s and returned to Lebanon with greater combat experience and international jihadi contacts, including with al Qaeda. Asbat al-Ansar has likely been receiving al Qaeda funds since the late 1990s and has become even more stridently anti-Western in its rhetoric since.

LINKS TO AL QAEDA: On September 25, 2001, Asbat al-Ansar released a statement that it was not allied with al Qaeda, while still praising bin Laden and his cause. In fact, the two have developed increasingly close ties since the late 1990s, with some Asbat al-Ansar members having gone to Afghanistan to attend al Qaeda training camps. After the beginning of the Global War on Terrorism, al Qaeda members are suspected of having sought refuge in Ayn al-Hilwah with Asbat al-Ansar. The group's al Qaeda links were significantly cited when it was listed among eleven groups whose assets were frozen by President Bush by executive order on September 23, 2001. The group's al Qaeda links were also prominently noted when the U.S. State Department designated Asbat al-Ansar as a foreign terrorist organization in March 2002.

ACTIVITIES AND ATTACKS SINCE 9/11: Although Asbat al-Ansar has conducted several low-level attacks since 9/11, the group has not managed to carry out a large-scale attack to date. In October 2001, Lebanese and Jordanian authorities disrupted an Asbat al-Ansar plot to attack the

U.S., Jordanian, and British embassies in Beirut. Since then, the group has returned to its more common practice of attacking "un-Islamic" targets. In 2002, Asbat al-Ansar was believed to have carried out the bombings of three Western fast-food restaurants. The group was involved in a foiled assassination plot against the U.S. ambassador to Lebanon, Vincent Battle, while he was visiting Tripoli in January 2003, that would have involved firing an armor-piercing missile at the ambassador's car. Similarly, Asbat al-Ansar associates were involved in an April 2003 failed car bomb attack against a McDonald's restaurant in a suburb of Beirut and a June rocket attack against the Future TV building in Beirut later that year. Additionally, some Asbat al-Ansar members are suspected of traveling to Iraq to fight the U.S.-led coalition, possibly with the help of al Qaeda associate Abu Mus'ab al-Zarqawi. Prior to the start of the war in Iraq, Zarqawi is also suspected of having traveled to the Ayn al-Hilwah camp to establish contacts for future joint operations.

OUTLOOK AND FUTURE INDICATORS: Although Asbat al-Ansar has not yet successfully conducted a major anti-U.S. or anti-Western attack, group members have the intent to do so as well as access to explosives and weaponry. The group has had a rather ineffectual terrorist track record compared to other Sunni extremist groups, but the fact that Asbat al-Ansar continues to maintain links to al Qaeda and Zarqawi make it more likely that access to this expertise will increase the group's capabilities and the potential lethality of its attacks.

NORTH AFRICAN ISLAMIC EXTREMIST NETWORK IN EUROPE

GROUP LEADER(S): None

CURRENT SIZE: Unknown

HISTORY: North Africans, and predominantly Moroccans and Algerians, make up a significant portion of the Muslim population in most of the countries in western and southern Europe. Morocco and Algeria are also a main center of the Takfiri Sunni ideology, in which all non-Muslims as well as Shia Muslims are considered apostates and it is considered the duty of all true Muslims to participate in jihad against them. Takfiri extremists with experience in the Bosnian or Chechen jihads of the 1990s, including members of Morocco's Salafiya Jihadiya, are able to recruit from among western and southern Europe's population of unemployed or low-income Muslim youth who feel disenchanted with European society and its latent anti-immigrant sentiments. Members of the missionary group Takfir wa al-Hijra and Jamaat al-Tabligh conduct similar activities to radicalize moderate Muslims. Al Qaeda at times has also been able to tap into this same vulnerable Muslim population.

Links to al Qaeda: Some extremist cells disrupted in Europe have had clear al Qaeda links, while others, such as the Madrid bombers, appear to have formed the attack plots on their own. The core group of al Qaeda's 9/11 attack cell was based in Germany. Abu Mus'ab al-Zarqawi has maintained links to North African contacts in Europe as well, and some North African extremists maintain links to associates in Chechnya.

Activities and Attacks Since 9/11: Some North African extremists in Europe have been involved in several foiled plots in several countries, while others have provided logistical support for extremists elsewhere in South Asia, the Middle East, and Africa. In April 2002, German authorities arrested nine members of al-Tawhid, a Zarqawi-founded group committed to killing Jews and establishing an Islamic state in Jordan, for their activities as a support cell for extremists operating against coalition forces in Afghanistan. In September, Dutch authorities arrested twelve North Africans who were recruiting young Muslims and providing them with stolen or forged passports to send them to jihad in an unknown country. In November, six North Africans were arrested in London for planning to conduct a possible cyanide gas attack, probably against the London subway system. U.K. authorities noted that at the time of arrest, no gas or hazardous material was found and the attack was likely in its early planning stages.

During the period December 24–27, 2002, a series of nine arrests in France uncovered a plot by North African extremists to bomb the Russian Embassy in Paris on behalf of Chechen associates. In January 2003, eight men were arrested in London, disrupting a plot to conduct a ricin attack in the United Kingdom. Spain subsequently arrested sixteen North Africans who had suspicious materials that were likely related to the ricin plot in the United Kingdom. In late January, Italian authorities disrupted an apparent plot by North Africans to attack the North Atlantic Treaty Organization (NATO) base in Verona, Italy. In a major successful attack, Moroccan extremist members of the Moroccan Islamic Combatant Group (GICM), with assistance from a cell of the Moroccan-based Salafiya Jihadiya, detonated time bombs on four commuter trains in Madrid, Spain, in early March 2004, killing 191 people and wounding more than 1,900. In late March, British authorities arrested eight men with links to the radical group al-Muhajiroun, who had half a ton of ammonium nitrate fertilizer and possibly planned to detonate it in combination with highly toxic osmium tetroxide against unknown targets. On June 9, Italian officials arrested Egyptian extremist and Madrid train attack mastermind Rabei Osman Sayed Ahmed. His arrest led French officials to arrest on June 15 twelve North Africans who were possibly planning to bomb the Paris subway system.

OUTLOOK AND FUTURE INDICATORS: The disaffected North African Muslim population in Europe will remain vulnerable to recruitment to extremist causes for the foreseeable future. There does not appear to be any indication of a near-term change in the anti-immigrant biases and protectionist government policies of the majority of most Western European countries. The true danger of these cells is that they can form quickly and conduct relatively inexpensive attacks without the need to travel and attend terrorist training camps outside of Europe. This will continue to make it difficult for European intelligence agencies to identify the cells in their early stages. The availability of bomb-building manuals on the Internet also makes it increasingly easy for members of these small cells to prepare mass casualty attacks.

SOUTH AND CENTRAL ASIA

CHECHEN EXTREMISTS

The three most prominent Chechen extremists groups are: the Islamic International Brigade (IIB); Riyadus-Salikhin Reconnaissance and Sabotage Battalion of Chechen Martyrs (also known as Riyadus-as-Saliheen, or RAS); and the Special Purpose Islamic Regiment (SPIR).

GROUP LEADER(S): The U.S. State Department maintains that Shamil Basayev is the head of IIB, RAS, and SPIR. Basayev is also thought to lead several other extremists groups in the Caucasus: the Battalion of Kamikaze Shahid, the Congress of Peoples of Ichkeria and Dagestan, and the United Force of Caucasian Mujahideen. Aslan Maskhadov, former Chechen president and general, is believed to maintain a role in several Chechen extremists groups. Other important leaders include Doku Umarov (field commander), and Khamzat (a SPIR commander). Saudi extremist Abdel Aziz al-Gamdi, a.k.a. Abu Walid, the leader of the IIB and likely head of foreign extremists in Chechnya, was killed in a Russian air strike in mid-April 2004.

CURRENT SIZE: Exact numbers are not known, but RAS is reputed to have approximately 200 fighters and SPIR about 400 active fighters. Many of the fighters mix between the three main groups, so approximating their total strength is difficult.

HISTORY: Russia has waged two long wars against Chechen separatists in the past ten years. The first lasted from 1994 to 1996 and left the region in de facto independent status. In 1999, Chechen rebels launched incursions and bombings in neighboring regions, such as Dagestan, and carried out a series of bombings against apartment buildings in Moscow that killed over 300 people. Russia sent a large military force into Chechnya and has been battling the separatists and their terrorist allies in Chechnya since.

Russia has managed to control Chechnya's northern flatlands but has been unable to control the capital, Grozny, or the southern regions of Chechnya. Most of the war has consisted of guerrilla style, hit-and-run attacks by Chechen forces, and Russian forces have typically retaliated with artillery and air strikes. Chechen groups have also relied on suicide bombings and hostage takings for ransom. Chechens have become notorious for using brutal attacks against soft targets, including deploying suicide bombers on commuter trains and planting explosives on tracks near crowded train stations. Chechen militants are also the only known terrorist group to have used a radiological device. In 1995, rebels planted a radiological bomb in a Moscow park but notified reporters and never detonated the device.

LINKS TO AL QAEDA: The U.S. State Department claims that IIB, RAS, and SPIR are associated with bin Laden and al Qaeda and designated them as terrorist groups in February 2003 by executive order. Russian president Vladimir Putin contends that Chechen rebels work in close coordination with al Qaeda and receive support from non-Chechen Islamic extremists. A former Chechen rebel leader, Samir Saleh Abdullah al-Suwailem (alias Ibn-ul-Khattab), who was killed by Russian security forces with a poisoned letter in 2002, worked with Basayev to secure weapons, money, and fighters from bin Laden in October 1999. Khattab, a Saudi-born militant, and bin Laden shared the goal of creating one Islamic state in the Caucasus. Beginning as early as 1995, Chechen rebels received training in Afghanistan, indoctrination through Wahhabist schools throughout Chechnya, and millions of dollars in aid. Some experts maintain that the Chechen guerrillas' contacts with Islamist terrorists altered their cause from one of national independence to one of anti-Western holy war.

ACTIVITIES AND ATTACKS SINCE 9/11: Chechen rebels have conducted increasingly lethal attacks since 1999. According to Russian officials, the number of terrorist acts between 1999 and 2002 increased from 100 to 272. Almost all of the attacks since 2001 have been conducted using suicide bombers. In late October 2002, forty Chechen militants seized the Dubroyka Theater in Moscow and took 800 hostages. The IIB, RAS, and SPIR worked together to stage the theater attack by sharing fighters, weapons, and tactics. Chechen extremists attacked the headquarters of the Russian-backed Chechen government in Grozny in late December 2002 using a suicide truck bomb, killing eighty people. In mid-May 2003, an unsuccessful assassination attempt with a suicide bomber against pro-Russian Chechen president Akhmad Kadyrov at a religious festival in Chechnya resulted in eighteen dead and 145 wounded. In early July, two female suicide bombers attacked a music concert at Tushino airfield in Moscow, killing sixteen people. In early August, a suicide car bomber attacked a Russian military hospital in Mozdok, Russia, killing fifty and wounding seventy-seven. In September and December, commuter trains in southern Russia carrying mostly students were bombed, killing dozens. In December 2003, Chechen militants began a major guerrilla campaign in the Russian internal Republic of Ingushetia.

In January 2004, Western intelligence services alleged that Chechens had been carrying out chemical weapons experiments in Chechnya. One man arrested in France, on suspicion of plotting a terrorist attack, was alleged to have received chemical weapons training in Georgia's Pankisi

Gorge, a notorious safe haven for Chechen extremists. In early February, bombs placed in Moscow's subway system killed forty-two people and wounded over 100. In early May 2004, Chechen militants assassinated Chechen president Akhmad Kadyrov and killed twenty-three others. In June 2004, 200 well-armed rebels raided three towns in Ingushetia and targeted the Interior Ministry building of the province, killing ninety-five people. Basayev has allegedly planned to attack more towns in Dagestan in a similar fashion to the Ingushetia attacks. Chechen extremists staged nineteen attacks against Russian military bases and checkpoints in early August. In mid-August, a Chechen suicide bomber failed in an assassination attempt against acting Chechen president Sergei Abramov. On September 1, 2004, Chechen militants stormed a school in North Ossetia in southern Russia, taking 1,200 adults and children captive. It ended two days later with the deaths of at least 339 hostages, about half of them children. Although Maskhadov denies his connection to the massacre, Basayev proudly claimed responsibility for the raid and Russian officials claim that Maskhadov also played a role in the atrocity.

Outlook and Future Indicators for the Group: Chechen rebels have made two startling tactical shifts in the past two years. First, militants have shown an increased willingness to conduct "maximum casualty" attacks using suicide bombers against hard and soft targets. Second, rebels have opened up a new front against Russia in the republics of Dagestan and Ingushetia, which are mostly Muslim and full of Chechen refugees, and the group's latest maneuvers have taken the Russian military by surprise. Aslan Maskhadov announced on July 6, 2004, that he had enough guerrillas and firepower to fight Russian forces for the next twenty years and that he intended to assassinate whoever next assumed the Chechen presidency. He also stated that Chechen guerrillas would expand terror attacks further outside of Chechnya, likely with the use of suicide bombers.

Hizb-I Islami Gulbuddin (HIG)

Group Leader(s): Gulbuddin Hikmatyar is the founding leader of HIG. He is on the U.S. State Department's list of global terrorists and one of the FBI's "most wanted" terrorists. There is a $25-million bounty for Hikmatyar's capture.

CURRENT SIZE: Hikmatyar is suspected of having several hundred veteran fighters on call in Afghanistan and Pakistan, but the size of HIG is unknown.

HISTORY: Hikmatyar founded HIG in 1977 as a faction of the Hizb-I Islami Party, a fundamentalist Sunni group and a key mujahideen group in the Soviet-Afghan war. During the war, he became renowned for his brutal tactics, and when the Soviets pulled out of Afghanistan, he continued to fight other warlords for control of Kabul. HIG continued its rocket attacks on Kabul until March 1993, at which point Hikmatyar struck a deal with former enemy warlords and was named prime minister of Afghanistan. In the early 1990s, Hikmatyar ran several terrorist training camps in Afghanistan and began to send mercenary forces to other Islamic conflicts. HIG established deep ties to bin Laden, and Hikmatyar offered safe haven to bin Laden when he fled Sudan in 1996. In late 1996, the Taliban took power in Kabul, ousting the Rabbani government and forcing Hikmatyar to flee the capital.

LINKS TO AL QAEDA: The U.S. State Department has declared Hikmatyar a terrorist with ties to al Qaeda and contends that he is responsible for attacks on Afghans and foreigners. HIG has long-established ties to bin Laden, including Hikmatyar's offer of shelter to bin Laden in 1996. In concert with bin Laden, Hikmatyar has declared jihad against U.S.-led forces in Afghanistan and has condemned the presidency of Hamid Karzai. A raid in Kabul in April 2004 led to the arrest of eight men who had explosives, weapons, and documents that demonstrated their links to both Hikmatyar and al Qaeda.

ACTIVITIES AND ATTACKS SINCE 9/11: Since the beginning of Operation Enduring Freedom, Hikmatyar has coordinated his "holy war" against international forces in Afghanistan with Taliban and al Qaeda forces. HIG forces are suspected of a car bomb attack in Kabul in June 2003, which killed five people, including four German peacekeepers, and wounded thirty-one. In January 2004, Canadian soldiers raided a compound in Kabul, seizing weapons, drugs, and cash along with members of HIG. Hikmatyar is alleged to have plotted to assassinate the Afghan education minister, Yunus Qanooni, and the defense minister, Marshal Muhammad Qasim Fahim. He has also plotted to attack the American and NATO military headquarters. In March 2004, HIG forces were reported to have been involved in attacks on three U.S. military bases in southeastern Afghanistan. By July 2004, Hikmatyar had become even more active and is believed to have helped coordinate the regular attacks on police and government posts, nongovernmental organizations, elections workers, and relief workers that occurred in the run-up to the Afghan national election in October 2004. Similarly to al Qaeda and Taliban forces, HIG has benefited financially from the boom in opium trafficking in Afghanistan.

OUTLOOK AND FUTURE INDICATORS FOR THE GROUP: In April 2004, Hikmatyar called on fighters everywhere to fight U.S. and international forces in Afghanistan in similar fashion to the insurgents in Iraq. The group's increased cooperation with Taliban and al Qaeda forces and the "fertile" ground for guerrilla activities in Afghanistan seem to have given Hikmatyar and his HIG new life.

LASHKAR-E-TAYYIBA (LET)

GROUP LEADER(S): Hafiz Mohammad Saeed leads the Lashkar-e-Tayyiba (Army of the Pure), an extreme Sunni group based in Pakistan. In December 2001, he officially stepped down as the leader of LeT, likely in response to increased Pakistani pressure, and set up the front group Jamaat ad-Dawa. Although he stated that LeT would now be led by an eleven-member council, Saeed remained the leader of LeT. The group's military operations are led by Zaki-ur-Rahman Lakhvi, a Pakistani national who has commanded LeT's terrorist attacks in India since 1995.

CURRENT SIZE: LeT has between 1,000 and 3,000 members, with most based in the Pakistani province of Azad Kashmir and in the city of Muzaffarabad in northern Pakistan.

HISTORY: Founded in 1989, LeT is the militant wing of Markaz Dawa wal Irshad (MDI), a religious organization founded in 1987 that runs a center for Islamic teaching. LeT's goals are to return Indian Kashmir to Muslim control, incorporating it into Pakistani territory. It also advocates the overthrow of non-Muslim governments worldwide, echoing part of al Qaeda's ideology. The group is made up primarily of Pakistanis recruited from madrassas across the country. Although the group has primarily focused on fighting in Kashmir, the cadre of extremists who would later form LeT began their jihad experience during fighting against the Soviet Union in Afghanistan in the 1980s. During that time, group members formed links with what would later become al Qaeda, as well as with Pakistan's Inter-Services Intelligence Directorate (ISID). After the war ended, LeT links to both were maintained. The group began conducting operations in Kashmir beginning in 1993 and with ISID assistance has become one of the three largest and most lethal groups operating in the disputed territory. In Indian Kashmir, LeT has conducted many large mass-casualty attacks and assassinations, attacking Indian civilians in markets, police stations, airports, and border posts. LeT members also conducted a high-profile attack on an Indian army barracks at New Delhi's Red Fort in December 2000, in which three soldiers were killed and all of the attackers escaped. LeT funds its large organization through extensive real estate holdings in Pakistan, contributions from Pakistani sympathizers, and, it is believed, from Middle Eastern donors and al Qaeda.

LINKS TO AL QAEDA: Having maintained connections with al Qaeda members since the end of the Afghan War, LeT members have likely trained in al Qaeda training camps in Afghanistan. LeT has probably received some level of funding from bin Laden and likely provided al Qaeda members with safe houses and protection after operatives were forced to flee to Pakistan following the loss of al Qaeda's Afghan safe haven in late 2001. Of note, al Qaeda senior lieutenant Abu Zubaydah was captured at a LeT safe house in Faisalabad in March 2002. Following al Qaeda's dispersal and setbacks, LeT has been noted sending funds to pro–al Qaeda groups such as the Southeast Asian group Jemaah Islamiya. LeT operatives have also reportedly traveled to fight in Iraq, though it is currently unknown whether support for al Qaeda was one of their reasons for being sent. Separately, in June 2003 a federal grand jury in Alexandria, Virginia, charged eleven men for conspiring with LeT to engage in jihadist activity. After four of the men pled guilty to conspiracy and gun charges, the rest were reindicted for conspiracy to provide material support to al Qaeda and the Taliban.

ACTIVITIES AND ATTACKS SINCE 9/11: LeT has been involved in several high-profile, anti-Indian attacks since the 9/11 attacks. In mid-December 2001, a joint group probably comprising LeT and separatist group Jaish-e-Mohammed members attacked the Indian Parliament building in New Delhi. Although the attackers were all killed and did not succeed in killing any parliamentarians, the attack showed the brazen nature of LeT attacks and led to increased Indo-Pakistani tensions. LeT was subsequently banned by Pakistan in January 2002, and all Kashmiri terrorist groups lost almost all of their ISID assistance. LeT has also been banned in Canada, the United Kingdom, and the EU as well. President Bush designated LeT as a foreign terrorist organization in October 2001. In response, LeT renamed itself Jamaat ad-Dawa (Party of Preachers), though the group's membership and goals were unchanged. LeT leader Hafiz Mohammad Saeed also officially resigned as head of the group, but he still appears to run it from behind the scenes. LeT, along with other Kashmiri extremist groups, claimed responsibility for the killing of Kashmir law minister Mushtaq Ahmed Lone on September 11, 2002. Though it did not claim responsibility, Indian authorities believe that LeT was behind two timer-detonated car bomb attacks in the commercial district of Mumbai, India, near U.S. Consulate Mumbai in late August 2003 that killed fifty-two people and wounded 153. If LeT is responsible, this would represent the first use of car bombs by the group and would increase the lethality of attack options open to it for future operations.

OUTLOOK AND FUTURE INDICATORS: LeT leaders have been careful to maintain that their goals are focused on the ejection of India from Indian Kashmir, but the group's actions, especially after 9/11, are becoming increasingly supportive of al Qaeda. It is likely that the group will continue to carry out the majority of its attacks in Kashmir, but it may conduct more activities to support al Qaeda as the harassed al Qaeda network leans more heavily on it for logistics and aid.

LASHKAR-E-JHANGVI (LEJ)

GROUP LEADER(S): Muhammad Ajmal, a.k.a. Akram Lahori, is thought to be the radical Wahhabi Sunni group LeJ's current leader, though he is in Pakistani custody. Lahori and Riaz Basra were the group's co-founders, though Pakistani forces killed Basra in May 2002 and Lahori was captured in Karachi in June 2002 and was sentenced to death in April 2003. Senior LeJ member Qari Ataur Rahman, a.k.a. Naeem Bukhari, who was allegedly involved in the murder of Daniel Pearl, was also arrested in Karachi in 2002. Almost all of the group's leaders are veterans of the war in Afghanistan in the 1980s.

CURRENT SIZE: LeJ has a current strength of approximately 100 operatives. LeJ once had a much larger membership and sent operatives to fight with the Taliban regime against the Northern Alliance. Crackdowns by successive Pakistani governments have reduced the group's strength.

HISTORY: Lashkar-e-Jhangvi (LeJ) was founded in 1996 in Pakistan as a splinter group of the Wahhabi sectarian group Sipah-e-Sahaba Pakistan (SSP), which it said was not extreme enough. The group is named after SSP co-founder Maulana Haq Nawaz Jhangvi, who was killed in 1990. Both groups have been responsible for attacks on Shia targets in Pakistan, and LeJ has also been involved in anti-Western attacks in Pakistan and anti-Indian attacks in Kashmir. LeJ's goals are to overthrow the current Pakistani government in favor of a radical Sunni Islamic government and to create sectarian strife toward that end by targeting Pakistan's minority Shia community. The group is also virulently anti-Western. Press reports indicate that LeJ is organized in a loosely coordinated cell structure based primarily in the Punjab and several cities, including Faisalabad, Peshawar, and Karachi. A LeJ cell in Lahore conducted a failed assassination attempt in January 1999 against former Pakistani prime minister Nawaz Sharif and his brother, the chief minister of Punjab Province. A bomb that had been placed under a bridge his convoy would cross went off prematurely, killing three people.

LeJ's leadership was close to the Taliban regime, which offered group members sanctuary in Afghanistan, even after President Pervez Musharraf officially banned LeJ in August 2001 and demanded that the Taliban hand over any group members in its territory. Leading up to the September 11 attacks, LeJ operatives also established strong relationships with al Qaeda members in Afghanistan. Like al Qaeda, LeJ likely receives funding from Saudi Wahhabi donors in the Middle East and may receive funding from al Qaeda as well.

LINKS TO AL QAEDA: Following the fall of the Taliban in late 2001, LeJ operatives actively assisted al Qaeda members fleeing into Pakistan with safe houses and logistics. LeJ actively began to work on al Qaeda's behalf soon after. The two collaborated in the murder of Daniel Pearl, and al Qaeda apparently provided funds for LeJ to carry out the mid-

2002 attacks on French military contractors in Karachi and Consulate Karachi. LeJ's close links and assistance to al Qaeda were listed as central reasons it was designated a foreign terrorist organization by the U.S. State Department in January 2003.

ACTIVITIES AND ATTACKS SINCE 9/11: LeJ has carried out several anti-Western attacks, as well as mass-casualty attacks against Shia targets since the September 11 attacks. In October 2001, LeJ members attacked a Church of Pakistan service in Rahawalpur that resulted in sixteen Protestant dead. In March 2002, LeJ members conducted a grenade attack on a Protestant church in Islamabad. The attack resulted in five dead and forty-six wounded, including two Americans killed and thirteen wounded. LeJ also conducted several car bomb attacks. In May 2002, a suicide car bomber attacked a Pakistani Navy shuttle bus carrying French contractors, killing twelve people, including eleven French, and wounding nineteen, including eleven French. A June 14, 2002, suicide car bomb attack against the U.S. Consulate Karachi resulted in eleven deaths and fifty-one wounded. In a press conference after the attack, Pakistan's interior minister indicated that evidence pointed to LeJ, with al Qaeda assistance, as the perpetrators of both attacks. He also stated that LeJ had a role in the kidnapping and execution of *Wall Street Journal* reporter Daniel Pearl in late January 2002.

LeJ has also carried out significant attacks against Shia worshipers, including a June 8 attack on a police vehicle in Baluchistan Province that killed twelve Shia police recruits, a July 4, 2003, attack against Shia worshipers at a mosque in Quetta, which resulted in fifty-three dead and sixty-five wounded, and a March 2, 2004, attack on a procession of Shia worshipers in Quetta, in which attackers used machine guns and grenades to kill fifty-one and wound 154. In June 2004, Dawood Badini, the head of LeJ's Baluchistan Province cell that carried out both attacks, was captured in Karachi, but he has not yet been tried.

OUTLOOK AND FUTURE INDICATORS: LeJ has become a significant al Qaeda ally in Pakistan. The group, through its various cells, will likely continue to protect al Qaeda members with safe houses and forged travel documents, and it would be willing to carry out more attacks against Western targets on al Qaeda's behalf. Despite the capture of LeJ leader Akram Lahori and Baluchistan Province cell leader Badini, other LeJ cells in the country can continue their activities without any adverse effects from their arrests. No new overall leader appears to have been chosen while Lahori is in prison.

ISLAMIC MOVEMENT OF UZBEKISTAN (IMU)

GROUP LEADER(S): Tohir Yuldashev is a founder of the IMU and is the group's current leader based in Pakistan. Group cofounder Juma Namangani served as the head of military operations until his death in late 2001.

CURRENT SIZE: The group likely has 300–800 members. The IMU used to have a significantly larger membership of several thousand, primarily based in Afghanistan, and with a presence in Uzbekistan and Tajikistan; crackdowns by Central Asian governments and heavy IMU losses incurred during fighting against U.S.-backed Afghan forces in late 2001 has reduced those numbers.

HISTORY: The IMU was cofounded in 1998 by Islamic radicals Juma Namangani, who had Soviet military experience in Afghanistan, and Mullah Tohir Yuldashev. The two men split off from the Islamic Renaissance Party (IRP) of Uzbekistan because it was not radical enough for them. The two formed their own group, Adolat (Justice) and called for an Islamic revolution in Uzbekistan. As a result of the subsequent ban on Adolat and the arrest of two dozen group members by President Islam Karimov's government in 1992, Yuldashev and Namangani fled to Tajikistan from Uzbekistan and joined the IRP of Tajikistan. The IMU's goal when it formed in 1998 was to overthrow the secular government of Uzbekistan and replace it with an Islamic state. While Namangani served as the group's military leader, Yuldashev served as a key fund-raiser, traveling to the Middle East and Pakistan during the late 1990s, reportedly becoming closely associated with Pakistan's ISID. Yuldashev also met with Chechen commanders during the first Chechen war of 1994–1996. Namangani fought in the Tajik civil war until it ended in 1997 and then moved his base of operations and fighters into Afghanistan in 1997 after befriending the Taliban.

After the IMU's creation in Kabul under Yuldashev and Namangani's co-leadership, group members received training in camps run by al Qaeda. In February 1999, the IMU set off five remotely detonated car bombs in the Uzbek capital of Tashkent, killing sixteen people. IMU members also crossed from Afghanistan into the Ferghana Valley of southern Uzbekistan to conduct bombings against Uzbek government targets in 1999 and 2000. The IMU also kidnapped several groups of Western tourists during the same time period, though most escaped or were released, at times after a payment of ransom. Due in part to these kidnappings, the IMU was designated a foreign terrorist organization by the U.S. State Department in September 2000.

LINKS TO AL QAEDA: Yuldashev and Osama bin Laden have had close ties since the late 1990s. IMU forces fought alongside al Qaeda during fighting in Afghanistan in late 2001. IMU forces appear to have closely integrated themselves with al Qaeda associates in the tribal areas from late 2001 to the present. Further, IMU forces have been heavily engaged in fighting with Pakistani forces conducting operations in the tribal areas in the spring and summer of 2004, and IMU forces have reportedly taken heavy casualties. From details of the fighting, it appears that Arab al Qaeda members have chosen to flee from fighting rather than fight Pakistani forces. It is uncertain whether the IMU members are fighting to protect al Qaeda leaders in the area.

ACTIVITIES AND ATTACKS SINCE 9/11: In late 2001, the IMU's Afghan infrastructure and a large number of its members were killed during air strikes and in combat with U.S.-backed Afghan forces during the early stages of Operation Enduring Freedom. After Namangani was killed, Yuldashev and his remaining forces fled across the Pakistani border. They have largely remained in the tribal areas along the Afghan-Pakistan border, sheltering with al Qaeda and Taliban associates based there. The IMU is likely responsible for an attack against a Western Union office in Osh, Kyrgyzstan, in early May 2003. Kyrgyz authorities disrupted an IMU plot to bomb the U.S. Embassy and a hotel used by Westerners in Bishkek during the same time frame.

In late March 2004, an accidental explosion at a safe house in Bukhara, Uzbekistan, led police to uncover and disrupt the activities of additional operatives in Bukhara. Other operatives in Tashkent, including several female suicide bombers, subsequently carried out suicide attacks primarily against Uzbek police, while others blew themselves up rather than giving themselves up after Uzbek police surrounded their safe houses and engaged in firefights with those inside. Amid the terrorist attacks and police assaults on safe houses, nineteen people were killed and twenty-six wounded during fighting on March 28–29; another twenty-three people died and five were wounded on March 30. Both the IMU and a previously unknown group calling itself Islamic Jihad Group (IJG) claimed credit for the attacks. The IJG said in a statement that it carried out the attack because of the secular nature of the Uzbek regime and due to Uzbekistan's support for U.S.-led coalition efforts in Afghanistan. On July 30, three male suicide bombers blew themselves up at the U.S. and Israeli embassies and the Uzbek prosecutor's office in Tashkent. The attacks took place at the same time that trials began for fifteen operatives who had been arrested for the March attacks. Again, both the IMU and the IJG claimed responsibility.

OUTLOOK AND FUTURE INDICATORS: It remains unclear whether the IJG is a splinter group that separated from the IMU or is instead the IMU using another name to claim credit for the two Uzbek attacks to take pressure off itself. If it is a separate group, it is unclear whether its base is in Uzbekistan or Pakistan. Similarly, if it is responsible, the IJG track record of suicide attacks is likely to continue until key leaders are arrested or killed. Pakistani forces reportedly wounded IMU leader Yuldashev during fighting in the spring of 2004, and it is unclear whether he remains in the tribal areas of Pakistan along the Afghan border or has moved elsewhere. Were Yuldashev to die, there does not appear to be a clear successor to him in the group, and it is unknown whether the IMU would remain intact without him.

JAMAAT AL-TABLIGH (JT)

GROUP LEADER(S): Unknown

CURRENT SIZE: JT (Society for the Propagation of Islam), which is concentrated primarily in Pakistan, has thousands of adherents, some of whom are also in the Middle East, Europe, and North America.

HISTORY: Founded in India in 1927, Jamaat al-Tabligh is one of the largest conservative missionary movements in the world. Slowly spreading from South Asia, JT members can now be found worldwide. The movement is dedicated to the purification of Muslims by returning to the practices of the Prophet Muhammad in the seventh century. They call for the rejection of the modern world, preaching both in mosques and door-to-door in cities and towns. The movement advocates the segregation of women, is nonviolent, and is staunchly apolitical, refusing to discuss or take a stance on any modern events. Despite this, some in the movement evidently argued that the Taliban regime in Afghanistan was a perfect form of government. The movement's preachers attempt to recruit Muslim men, especially ones without strong religious beliefs looking for an identity, to travel and preach with them. In the United States, al Falah mosque in Queens, New York City, serves as a center of JT activity and hosted a gathering of 200 Canadian and American JT missionaries in 2003.

LINKS TO AL QAEDA: U.S. law enforcement officials have stated that JT teachings adhere to the extreme message of al Qaeda and other Islamic groups. Prior to the September 11 attacks, al Qaeda members also allegedly traveled in the guise of JT preachers, looking for good candidates to recruit from those they meet. Similarly, al Qaeda members have used the cover of traveling for JT as a reason given to receive visas issued and to have old airline tickets reissued. John Walker Lindh traveled with JT missionaries soon after he converted to Islam in 1999. He received assistance from a JT missionary to enroll in a madrassa in Pakistan to study Islam. From there, he traveled to a training camp in Afghanistan. An al Qaeda member, Kamal Derwish, recruited six Yemeni-American men from Lackawanna, New York, to travel to Pakistan in the spring of 2001. He instructed them to use the cover story that they were going to study Islam under JT missionaries. Once they arrived in Pakistan, they traveled on to Afghanistan and attended al Qaeda training camps. They were arrested in Lackawanna after returning to the United States, where they pled guilty to terrorism-related charges.

ACTIVITIES SINCE 9/11: Although no JT members are known to have been involved in any extremist activities, several cases since September 11 involve Islamic extremists in America attempting to use JT to help advance their activities. In late 2001, seven people from Portland, Oregon, tried to travel to Afghanistan to fight for the Taliban. Most returned after spending time in China, but Jeffrey Battle traveled on to Bangladesh with the intention of finding a JT missionary who could help him get military training and travel to fight for the Taliban. Islamic convert Iyman Faris, a truck driver who traveled to Afghanistan in 2000, used the cover of being a JT missionary to get old airline tickets reissued in late 2001 that were not originally in his name. When he returned to the United States, he studied attack plans with ultralight aircraft and worked on a plan to cut suspension cables on the Brooklyn Bridge on behalf of al Qaeda attack planner Khalid Shaikh Muhammad. Faris was arrested in early 2003.

OUTLOOK AND FUTURE INDICATORS: Although JT will likely continue to be a nonviolent missionary movement, al Qaeda and associated Islamic extremist groups will continue to use it as cover to travel and conduct recruiting and operational activities.

OTHER

HIZB'UT TAHRIR (HT)

GROUP LEADER(S): unknown

CURRENT SIZE: The group has between 10,000 and 100,000 adherents concentrated in twenty-five countries in Central Asia, the Middle East, Australia, North America, and several Central European countries. In the West, it is highly visible in the United Kingdom. A separate leadership structure in Indonesia claims to lead the "official" HT, and differences continue between it and the U.K. leadership, which all HT members in Western countries look to for guidance.

HISTORY: Hizb'ut Tahrir (HT) was founded in 1952 by Palestinian Taqi al-Din al-Nabhani as an offshoot of the militant Muslim Brotherhood. HT advocates the nonviolent overthrow of Muslim regimes that have been corrupted by Western influences. The group's long-term goal is to create an Islamic state that includes all of the Middle East and Central Asia to be ruled by Sharia law. HT focuses entirely on the political issue of changing the governments of "corrupted" Muslim states and has thus been outlawed in Pakistan, Russia, Germany, Turkey, and most countries in Central Asia. In the United States, the group is concentrated in California. Focused on political change and as a polar opposite of Wahhabist groups, HT does not restrict its members' dress, appeals to all denominations of Islam, and encourages the use of technology to proselytize and expand HT's membership. In Western society, members wear modern clothing. The group operates a significant number of propaganda Web sites designed to augment speaking rallies and media releases in promoting its agenda. Although these efforts are left to overt members of the group, other members work directly in Muslim communities to attempt to draw new members. Membership has increased since the early 1990s as Middle Eastern issues flared and several Central Asian governments, especially Uzbekistan, cracked down on Islamic groups operating in their countries. In recent years, several European governments, including those of Turkey and Germany, have also cracked down on the group and banned HT for its radical statements.

LINKS TO AL QAEDA: Although links between HT and al Qaeda appear at most to be indirect, Western officials have voiced concern over the similar goals the two share in overthrowing "Western" Muslim governments and establishing a pan-Islamic, Sharia-governed state. Also similar to al Qaeda, HT advocates the use of suicide bombers to attack Israel and has stated that occupying forces in Muslim lands can face the use of force to evict them. HT has not issued threats against U.S. forces in Saudi Arabia and Iraq, but the threat is implied. Also, HT leaders maintain ties to al-Muhajiroun, an HT splinter group that supported armed, violent action in jihad. Both al Qaeda members Zaccharias Moussaoui and Richard Reid were introduced to al Qaeda through al-Muhajiroun. It is possible that some HT members have similar links to al Qaeda as al-Muhajiroun, but that has not been positively established.

ACTIVITIES SINCE 9/11: HT has not changed its profile following the September 11 attacks. Group members have continued to recruit from among young Muslims and have continued the heavy use of Internet propaganda. Resentment in the Muslim world of perceived heavy-handed U.S. actions in the Global War on Terrorism, including the war in Iraq, have likely expanded the group's recruitment base. The government of Uzbekistan has stated that HT is attempting to overthrow it. Following suicide attacks in Tashkent in March and July 2004, the Uzbek government quickly released statements arguing that HT, with

IMU assistance, was responsible. The group issued statements denying responsibility for the attacks but reiterated calls for the Uzbek government to be replaced.

OUTLOOK AND FUTURE INDICATORS: HT will likely continue to have a strong following and be able to continue to recruit young Muslims in Europe, the Middle East, and Central Asia. HT's focus on a mixed political and religious agenda will enable it to have a very wide appeal, especially in countries with oppressive governments or in regions where active conflict is occurring, such as the Middle East.

AL-MUHAJIROUN (ALM)

GROUP LEADER(S): Syrian sheikh Omar Bakri Mohammed leads al-Muhajiroun (The Immigrants) from its headquarters in the United Kingdom. Bakri is an ex Hizb'ut Tahrir member who advocates attacks on Western countries and against "Westernized" Muslim governments. He has connections to many terrorists, including Osama bin Laden. He is currently a judge in the Court of Sharia U.K. and has issued numerous religious rulings (fatwas) saying that it was allowable to kill former British prime minister John Major and current prime minister Tony Blair, but only while they were traveling in Muslim countries.

CURRENT SIZE: ALM likely has upward of 1,000 members, though the group's cell-based structure makes it difficult to determine the group's actual strength.

HISTORY: Al-Muhajiroun was founded in 1996 by Bakri after he left Hizb'ut Tahrir because of a dispute over the use of violence. ALM advocates the establishment of a pan-Islamic state based on Sharia law but also seeks to establish the rule of Sharia law wherever Muslims are present, even in Western society. The group is heavily based in the United Kingdom but also has a presence in the United States. Most members, who are heavily recruited from among the population of young Muslim men disaffected with Western society in the United Kingdom and United States, wear traditional clothing and beards. Due to the group's violent propaganda and Bakri's extremist contacts, ALM is thought to be a feeder of young recruits for al Qaeda, Hizbullah, and Asbat al-Ansar, though this has not been proven. It is thought that Bakri provided assistance to U.K.-based Muslims to travel to Afghanistan for training in al Qaeda camps in the 1990s. Bakri has repeatedly stated in his sermons that it is the duty of Muslims to fight and attack those who attack Muslims, and to strike Western countries. Despite this, ALM has not been banned in Britain due to the country's laws protecting free religion. Bakri has claimed that he recruited a suicide operative who attacked Indian soldiers in Kashmir in December 2000. In January 2001, another ALM-linked British citizen conducted another suicide attack against an Indian army barracks.

Links to al Qaeda: Bakri has a long association with Osama bin Laden. He issued bin Laden's decrees through his media sources in the 1990s and later praised the 9/11 hijackers. Bakri also assisted men traveling to Afghanistan for training and has praised bin Laden's anti-Western agenda.

Activities Since 9/11: Group members have been involved in a series of plots and attacks in recent years. Two British ALM members were identified as Hamas suicide bombers who attacked a bar in Tel Aviv in April 2003, killing three. In January 2003, U.K. authorities raided apartments around London in connection with arrests that indicated a plot to use ricin in an attack. Several North African suspects arrested in connection with the plot were linked to an ALM Web site. In the spring of 2004, suspects were arrested in London after police seized a warehouse containing 1,200 pounds of ammonium nitrate fertilizer associated with the suspects. Earlier in April, Bakri had issued a statement that a group called al Qaeda Europe would conduct an attack on London soon. The group's Pakistani branch separated from the U.K. headquarters in February 2004, arguing for a more moderate approach to achieve the group's goals.

Outlook and Future Indicators: ALM will likely continue to espouse violent and radical propaganda until key group leaders are arrested and its media outlets are closed. ALM members will likely continue to plan and carry out attacks or to support other groups by providing members and logistical support for attacks. Additionally, ALM members in the United States pose a potential threat to either conduct an attack in the United States or support other groups planning to do so.

4. A Country-by-Country Approach

The jihadists seek to overthrow existing governments in Islamic nations and replace them with Taliban-style theocracies or caliphates. Although the United States needs a broad strategy to counter the jihadists (both by arresting the individual terrorists and by appealing to the broader Islamic world), it must also develop country-by-country strategies. Tailoring tactics toward particular nations will help policymakers to think more systematically about the trade-offs and collateral effects associated with targeting particular circles within the concentric circles framework.

This chapter examines conditions in five nations in which the jihadists are either seeking to replace existing governments or have already succeeded in installing a fundamentalist regime. Those nations are Saudi Arabia, with the world's largest oil reserve; Egypt, with the largest Arab population; Iran, a non-Arab Islamic nation that supports terrorism and is believed to be actively seeking nuclear capability; Pakistan, a non-Arab Islamic nation with nuclear weapons; and Iraq, a country that faces the risk of descending into civil war in the wake of the U.S.-led ouster of Saddam Hussein.

This analysis explores the dimensions of democratization, stability, anti-Americanism, and jihadism in those countries with an eye toward assessing changes in the next five to seven years.

Although near-term radical change in the governments of most of these nations is not the most probable scenario, our lack of understanding of political, religious, and socioeconomic undercurrents in these countries means that we cannot rule out surprise shifts. The governance and economic systems in all of them are inherently unviable over the near to long term.

In 1979, the United States was surprised by the extent of the opposition to the Pahlavi government in Iran. Our surprise stemmed in part from our lack of independent sources of intelligence and our reliance upon the regime's reports of its own stability. Although the

U.S. government pledged after the fall of the shah not to be put in a similar situation in the future, it is the case that we lack adequate independent sources of information on the stability of most of these key countries.

Potential leadership changes will likely play a critical role in the future of all of these countries, particularly with regard to their stability and democratization in the long term.

For example, if jihadi extremists were to succeed in assassinating President Musharraf and thereby initiate a struggle for control of the state, that country's security would be less certain, and significant change and instability could be expected.

The prospect for democratization in these countries remains dim. In Egypt and Saudi Arabia, advances in democratization will most likely come in the form of minor or cosmetic liberalization of their political systems. At the same time, economic liberalization is likely to increase in Egypt along with economic diversification in Saudi Arabia—the consequences of such economic reform, however, are likely to increase the discontent of the citizenry and, therefore, to result in increased repression by the state. This atmosphere is not conducive to real democratic progress.

In Iran, a stalemate between conservatives and reformists, coupled with foreign security threats, is likely to overshadow efforts to bring democratization onto the political agenda. Iranian society has proved extremely patient and is likely to exhibit unity at a time when it faces significant international pressure related to its nuclear program and the changes taking place in neighboring Iraq. A similar situation exists in Pakistan, where President Musharraf's efforts, in spite of his rhetoric, seem to focus more on regime survival than substantive democratization.

Were democratic elections held today in many parts of the Islamic world, pro-jihadist candidates would likely be elected. That has already happened in the abortive Algerian election and in provincial elections in Pakistan. Polling shows 48 percent support for al Qaeda's goals and philosophy in Saudi Arabia. The risk is that such elections would be "one man (and perhaps only men), one vote, one time," followed by the institution of a nondemocratic theocratic system. Thus, it is as important to create the rules and conditions surrounding a true democratic process as it is simply to hold a vote. Such conditions include a prolonged period of unrestricted journalism and public education. They involve constitutional arrangements guaranteeing minority rights, rights that cannot be easily changed.

A deeper understanding of jihadism and anti-Americanism requires an appreciation for the way in which such phenomena vary from one country to another. Conventional approaches propose that anti-Americanism is a reaction to American policy in the region. Such calls to "take Arabs seriously" insist that a dialogue with Middle Eastern social elites, which results in a shift in American foreign policy, would significantly reduce the level of anti-Americanism in the region. Some Middle East experts argue, however, that U.S. policy in the Middle East has a much less significant impact on anti-Americanism in the region. Scholar Barry Rubin contends that "neither launching a public relations campaign nor changing Washington's policies will affect [anti-Americanism]."

As conventional explanations have become increasingly inadequate, determining the origins and objectives of anti-American movements and understanding how the movements are consistent and different across countries have become crucial. Whereas state-sanctioned anti-Americanism thrives in Egypt and Saudi Arabia, the state-sponsored anti-Americanism of Iran is detached from a population that is effectively pro-American. One common thread uniting anti-Americanism across the region is that it is propagated by various powerful interest groups within the countries.

It is likely that such ideological phenomena will have an impact on the progress of stability and democratization. If the forecast for progress remains dismal, then jihadism will continue to increase in Egypt and Saudi Arabia, and state-sanctioned anti-Americanism will heighten the likelihood of an insurgency. The Saudi regime will need to act swiftly to stem this impending social catastrophe. Anti-Americanism in Iran, propagated by the conservative regime, will continue to widen the gap between the regime and the population, further intensifying the call for democratization and serious political change.

In this chapter, we describe what we believe is the current state of affairs in these nations. We do not offer specific country-by-country strategies, which must be developed in detail by teams of experts on each nation, including nongovernment specialists. But in general, the strategies to be formulated must seek to persuade parties in these nations to engage in rapid but nonrevolutionary change, increasing participation in governance, expanding economic opportunity, strengthening public education, and encouraging democratic and civil societal forces. Increasing the status and rights of women is a key part of the overall effort to increase stability in these nations. The United States must have tailored, detailed, proactive, and integrated policies for enhancing stability and democratic forces in key Islamic nations. As part of this effort, the United States must develop its own reliable sources of information about domestic political, social, and security trends in these nations.

Because the U.S. government is widely disdained in these nations, nongovernmental organizations and other like-minded governments may have to take the lead in these efforts. The word "democracy" has often been misunderstood to mean "the American way," so it will often be necessary to describe democracy in other terms, building on existing historical, cultural, and religious concepts that favor openness and participation in governance.

SAUDI ARABIA

The fate of Saudi Arabia has long been the subject of scrutiny. In the heyday of Nasser-inspired pan-Arabism, many predicted the dissolution of Saudi Arabia in the face of pressure from then radical Arab regimes of Egypt, Iraq, and Syria. Similarly, the 1979 Iranian Revolution and glimmers of Islamist dissent in the 1980s prompted commentators to question the viability of the al Saud government in the Arabian Peninsula. All this, of course, took place in a context of declining oil revenues, rapid population growth, and the increasingly public fragmentation of interests and generations within the Saudi clan. This made for a dismal picture of Saudi Arabia's future. Yet a quarter of a century later, the al Saud still reign.

- **SUCCESSION:** Can the various factions within the Saudi clan agree upon a mechanism for future succession that will minimize tension within the family while maintaining its legitimacy within the kingdom?

- **ROLE OF THE CLERGY:** How will the relationship between the royal house and the religious establishment evolve?

Disputes between various factions over a legitimate mechanism for succession could prove destabilizing for Saudi Arabia. The issue of succession in Saudi Arabia is linked to the challenge of defining the role and power of the Wahhabi religious leaders. The precarious relationship between spiritual and temporal power forged over two centuries ago may now demand realignment. This will be the single most important determinant of anti-Americanism and jihadism in the coming years. Most critically, there has been an alignment of the violence-prone "bin Ladenist" agenda of groups like al Qaeda and the traditional Wahhabi religious establishment. Future rulers will have to find new ways of navigating between the puritanical demands of the Wahhabi clerics, the possibility of an enduring insurgency, and international pressure for democratization and economic reform. In the rhetoric of the extremist opposition—one that represents a departure from earlier patterns—the al Saud have been identified as a "backward" contingent to be expunged from Saudi Arabian society. Whether and how the al Saud can address all such challenges in a cohesive, and popularly legitimate fashion, will largely determine the prospects for stability in Saudi Arabia.

Who will rule? And how will they rule? Succession by the king's eldest son, known as primogeniture, has gradually become the guiding principle for succession in most Gulf countries, with the exception of Saudi Arabia.[1] Instead, the pattern there has been the succession of Ibn Saud's sons in order of their age and presumed fitness to rule (Saud, Faisal, Khaled, and the current King Fahd). Early on, in 1954, the Saudi monarch also took on the position of prime minister, assigning the office of deputy prime minister to the heir apparent. In 1967, an additional post of second deputy prime minister was created to include the heir to the heir apparent. The al Saud have historically been very conscious of the importance of publicly affirming the future of succession, although such public affirmations may have more to do with the need to appease or preempt ambitious throne-seekers than a desire to cultivate public support.

Thus, the ruling family has taken steps to institutionalize succession. In 1992, for example, King Fahd established the important precedent of publicly announcing Prince Abdullah as heir apparent. The 1992 Basic Law also established the power of the king to appoint or remove his heir apparent at will. These steps reflect al Saud recognition of the increasing difficulty of controlling the uncertainties surrounding the succession. Further complicating the succession process is the size of the Saudi ruling family, which has grown to nearly 5,000 princes, and the generational cleavages that exist alongside traditional tribal, historical, and ideological divisions within the Saudi clan.

Another threat to Saudi stability lies in the fragmentation of the ruling family itself. Speculation about the possibility of such a breakdown raises the question of whether any viable opposition actually exists in Saudi Arabia that could take advantage of such disorder. It is more likely that family elders, tribal leaders, and skillful negotiation (characteristic of the al Saud past) would prevent such fragmentation from making the family vulnerable. In the end, the critical imperative for all family members is to maintain al Saud control over the Saudi state. Therefore, it is unlikely that any threat to such essential goals will be tolerated from within the family.

Some observers have detected an emerging split within the family between Crown Prince Abdullah and Prince Nayef, both of whom are thought to represent distinctly different visions of Saudi Arabia's future. According to some assessments, Crown Prince Abdullah represents the liberal face of taqarub—rapprochement between Muslims and non-Muslims—and the expansion of the political community to include those that have traditionally been left out. Unencumbered by ties to the more corrupt members of the Saudi family, Abdullah's rule is seen as more conducive to promoting democratic reform, as demonstrated by his key role in the recent "national dialogue" with Saudi liberals and Shiites.

On the other side of the spectrum is the conservative interior minister, Prince Nayef, who is said to embrace more fully the Wahhabi conception of *tawhid*, or monotheism, as central to Saudi identity and the legitimacy of the royal house. At the heart of *tawhid* is a conception of jihad aimed not only against non-Muslims but also against non-Wahhabi Muslims. Prince Nayef's priority is to bolster the support of the religious leaders, known as the ulema, for the Al Saud by ensuring their unique authority over the boundaries of Islamic belief and practice within the kingdom and their perceived responsibility for propagating Wahhabism in the rest of the world. By supporting the struggle of the Wahhabi clerics against the West, against liberal reformers, and against religious minorities within Saudi Arabia, Prince Nayef seeks to reinforce the stability of the al Saud as the ruling political authority. The flaw in this arrangement lies in the intensifying connection between the ulema and violent extremists.

The war in Iraq has sparked a new wave of jihadist insurgency in Saudi Arabia. One insurgent group, calling itself the Fallujah Brigade of a larger group known as "al Qaeda in the Arabian Peninsula," claimed responsibility for the kidnapping and beheading of Paul Johnson, a Lockheed Martin employee. The leader of the Fallujah Brigade, Abdulaziz

Muqrin, also claimed a role in ongoing campaigns in Iraq. Such jihadist organizations proclaim the goal of pushing the "infidels" out of Arab lands. The Saudi government has only recently recognized the threat posed by militant jihadism and begun acting to thwart an insurgency. With twelve out of twenty-six major suspects apprehended, Saudi security officials claim to have disrupted the five major cells in Saudi Arabia. The insurgency, however, continues to attract a younger generation of militant Saudis who, unlike their older counterparts, were not part of the campaign in Afghanistan. Instead, many have returned from exploits in Iraq and are now directing their energies at the al Saud.

Political reform has become a casualty of the regime's struggle against jihadists. With the sanction of the religious leaders, the al Saud are facing off against extremists and, in exchange, the al Saud have been reluctant to push for any type of social and political reform that threatens the esteemed position of the ulema.

Crown Prince Abdullah's accession to the throne would bring little real change to the system. This is not to say that Abdullah will lack allies: Saudi liberals are likely to support him for his inclinations for reform, while some Wahhabi clerics will continue to rate him highly for his commitment to a Bedouin lifestyle in the face of the massive corruption and scheming of the more dominant factions of his family. At the same time, the reforms that Abdullah may seek to carry out are likely to anger a large segment of the ulema, especially if such reforms are seen to represent a rupture with the tradition of the past or the powers of the ulema.

Crown Prince Abdullah, indeed, has done little to implement political reforms. For example, the government announced in Ocober 2004 that women would not be allowed to vote or run for office in municipal elections now scheduled to be held in three stages from February 10 to April 21.

Most likely, the government will continue to crack down on extremists with the support of the ulema in exchange for leaving women's rights, education, and the international momentum of Wahhabism off the reform agenda. Democratization is likely to be met with opposition from the ulema, who will correctly see any step toward democracy as a threat to their ability to ensure that the standards of pious living continue to guide public and private life within the kingdom. Meanwhile, Saudi citizens lament the current state of economic reform and they see little sign that anything will improve. In a 2002 poll by Zogby International, 67 percent of Saudis aged eighteen to twenty-nine indicated that they felt they were better off economically than their children ever would be.

The growing influence of Islam in Saudi Arabia has had a significant impact on the kingdom, with numerous implications for democratization and stability. Whereas older Saudis generally identify themselves first as Arabs, the younger generation prefers identification by religion. Only 14 percent of Saudis aged thirty and older preferred to identify themselves as Muslims first, in comparison to 35 percent for Saudis between the ages of eighteen and twenty-nine. Interestingly, Saudi women are also a reservoir of conservatism, with 27 percent preferring to define themselves first by religion in contrast to only 17 percent for men.

The early 1990s marked a series of initiatives by the al Saud to counter the effects of Islamization within the military and society at large. The Ministry of Islamic Affairs was created to oversee Islamic discourse in sermons and Saudi Arabia's universities. In October 1994, the Majlis al-Da'wa (Religious Propagation Council) was established and given the power to oversee and standardize Friday sermons as well as take a role in designing educational programs. The Islamization of the National Guard may prove a threat to the ruling family if its members stake out a path of reform targeting such issues as women's rights or the education system.

The crucial questions remain: Who will follow Crown Prince Abdullah, what type of society will Abdullah leave behind, and how much longer will it be until such a transition occurs? Given the age of Ibn Saud's sons and the ambition of the younger generations, the next ten to twenty years will most likely see the ascension to the throne of one of the younger cadres of the al Saud. The greatest gift the current elders could give to such a ruler—and the greatest contribution they could make to Saudi stability and the prospects for democratization—would be to create a legitimate process by which rulers will succeed to the throne. How such a ruler will meet the challenges of anti-Americanism and jihadism, however, is a far more complex question.

Anti-Americanism and jihadism in Saudi Arabia are inextricably linked and skillfully manipulated by key players. Unlike in Egypt where, for example, regime-sponsored anti-Americanism seeks to deflect the public's attention from government abuses, anti-American posturing in Saudi Arabia would provide political contenders with a means to demonstrate to the ulema their commitment to the status quo. For ambitious members of the al Saud clan eager to move up the ladder, a reputation for anti-Americanism would signal to the ulema their opposition to reforms that would threaten the position of the ulema. Prince Nayef's self-conscious anti-Americanism and his widely known lack of enthusiasm for the American approach to the war on terrorism has earned him the esteem of the ulema. Essentially, supporting America is tantamount to rocking the boat.

Although much of the Middle East views both the United States and American foreign policy unfavorably, Saudi Arabia consistently scores the highest in its anti-Americanism. Of a random sample of 700 individuals in Riyadh and Jeddah, only 4 percent had a favorable opinion of the United States, with 95 percent or more believing that the recent war with Iraq would bring less democracy and more terrorism. Ninety-seven percent of Saudis believe that U.S. policy in Iraq is influenced primarily by oil, in addition to American support for Israel. Such numbers are intriguing, given the history of close relations between Saudi and American elites.

Anti-Americanism in Saudi Arabia is fueled by resentment against liberals and prejudice against minority religious communities within the borders of Saudi Arabia. As one observer has put it, anti-Americanism in Saudi Arabia is a "product of self-interested manipulation by various groups within Arab society." This is not to say that some Saudi princes are not truly anti-American—indeed, the complexity of ideology within the family includes both Americophiles and the most ardent of anti-Americanists. Rather, religious and political authorities resort to anti-Americanism as an important tactic in their own efforts to secure their dominant positions within society. These authorities have skillfully used the U.S. occupation in Iraq and the newly prominent role of Shiites in Iraq to inflame anti-Americanism. Anti-Americanism, therefore, serves as a pretext for opposing forces of change within Saudi Arabia. Changes in U.S. policy will have little significant impact on the scope and quality of anti-Americanism.

EGYPT

Stability and authoritarian leadership have historically progressed hand in hand in Egypt. Understanding why stability and authoritarianism have been mutually reinforcing will be important as we try to appreciate how democratization will fit into Egypt's future. Does stability require that future Egyptian leaders continue the tradition of authoritarian tendencies shown by leaders who have followed Gamal Abdel Nasser? Given the recent buzz about the rapid rise of Hosni Mubarak's son, Gamal, and rumors of his eventual ascension to power, this is a timely question, especially in view of Gamal's promotion as a "liberal."

More important is the historically dominant role that the military has played in Egyptian politics. Gamel Abdel Nasser, Anwar Sadat, and current president Hosni Mubarak have each emerged from the ranks of the military to reign as Egypt's most powerful leader. Egypt relies heavily on powerful security services that are linked closely to the regime and dominate all aspects of life. Arbitrary jailing, the oppression of individuals, and the permanence of emergency laws all serve as reminders of the extensive law enforcement powers of security officials loyal to the regime. The enduring role of the military in civil affairs has left an imprint on Egyptian society, some segments of which are anxious about Gamal's ascension to power given his nonmilitary background.

At the same time, Egypt can be classified as relatively democratic when compared to its immediate neighbors. The courts are more independent, at times even ruling against the executive, as when in 1987, 1990, and 2000, the Supreme Constitutional Court declared the election of deputies to parliament to be unconstitutional, which forced new elections. The press enjoys a substantial amount of freedom, although it stops short of directly criticizing the president. Civil society and human rights organizations also enjoy a fairly vibrant set of freedoms, with approximately 16,000 civil society organizations registered in Egypt in 2003, including business associations, youth groups, clubs, political parties, and nongovernmental organizations.

The implications of reform in Egypt are hard to assess. A look at the effects of liberalization in the past suggests that reforms affecting wages, food prices, and rents can spur instability. In 1977, demonstrators in Cairo protested Sadat's reforms, which had sent the price of food staples soaring. Yet, reforms in the political realm are more likely to find favor. Democracy continues to be a broadly popular concept in Egyptian society and progress toward it—sponsored from within and not by outside actors—will be met with approval. Unlike Saudi Arabia, where the ulema stand to lose from the process of democratization, in Egypt no major sector of society—apart from the regime—is threatened by democratization. In fact, Islamist groups like the Muslim Brotherhood, whose ultimate objectives remain deliberately cloaked in ambiguity, would make serious gains if their informal support were translated into formal political power.

Mubarak's successor, however, is unlikely to back such reforms. Changes that have taken place thus far have been cosmetic, including Sadat's introduction of a formal multiparty political structure and Mubarak's electoral reform. Neither of these initiatives truly expanded the scope for political participation by Egyptian voters. Rather, the reforms were manipulated by the regime to strengthen itself while continuing to exclude potential competitors. Within Egypt, the anticipation of political change has been heightened by Mubarak's failing health, the impending end of his fourth term in office, and debates about democracy that now dominate the airwaves. Despite this yearning, it is unclear whether genuine political reform, if it were to happen, would result in the kind of democracy that Egyptian liberals—and Washington—wish for. Hopelessness, financial hardship, and an increasingly Islamist mindset have become as pervasive in Egypt as has longing for meaningful political expression. Those factors may be as much of a barrier to democratization as regime intransigence.

Egyptian observers of the post–Hosni Mubarak era have envisioned two succession scenarios: in one, Gamal Mubarak accedes to power, much as Bashar al Asad did, though as a determined liberalizer; in the other, Omar Suleiman, a senior army officer and long-serving intelligence chief, takes over, determined to preserve the status quo. The nature of Egypt's political system depends on the nature of the leader, so the question of succession is critical. Whatever the "true" nature of the candidates might be, the pressing question is whether either of them can be expected to maintain stability.

It appears now as if the ground is being carefully prepared for Gamal Mubarak's succession. His father has been doing all he can to ensure that Gamal will take office. The most recent Egyptian cabinet, formed in July 2004, is the first cabinet ever to include businessmen alongside a limited number of regime stalwarts. More controversial was the exit of two of Mubarak's longest-serving ministers, including old guard Information Minister Safwat al-Sherif. Nine out of thirty-four of the ministers sit on the Policy Committee, which itself is chaired by Gamal. Moreover, fourteen of them also have some sort of personal or business ties to Gamal. Led by the relatively obscure and inexperienced Ahmed Nazief, the mission of this new—and overwhelmingly young—cabinet is to focus exclusively on economic reform. To this end, Rashid Muhammad Rashid, a former senior executive at Unilever, has been brought in along with thirty-nine-year-old Mahmoud Mohiedin as head of a newly formed Ministry of Investment.

Gamal, in the meantime, has been careful not to rule out an interest in the presidency. If the transition from a Hosni Mubarak government to one led by Gamal takes place, it could set in motion serious political shifts that could ultimately pave the way for the increased participation of Islamists in Egyptian politics. The stakes are high. Bearing in mind the historical connection in Egypt between authoritarianism and stability, no one can say what will happen to stability if Gamal Mubarak jettisons his father's authoritarian style.

Gamal Mubarak's ascension is unlikely to produce immediate ruptures within Egyptian society. Most Egyptians will patiently wait to see what direction Gamal intends to take the country. Yet multiple uncertainties during the next five years will contribute to increasing instability. First, Gamal's ascension to the presidency will be seen as illegitimate by many Egyptians, regardless of the nature of the process. Moreover, America's embrace will only serve to increase Gamal's image as illegitimate and label him, in Egyptian opinion, as an American poodle.

Whether or not Egyptian commentators are right about Gamal's supposed liberalism, conditions for instability are likely to grow within the first two years of his presidency. At least three trends will encourage instability: the increasingly Islamist outlook of the population, the millennialism associated with the current political moment, and the financial burdens on an already despairing population that are likely to result from Gamal's expected economic reforms.

These factors could lead to instability along two separate paths. First, Gamal's introduction of substantive political reforms could open the political process to the opposition. Although political reforms would boost Gamal's popularity at home, while appeasing international pressure for reform, these positive outcomes would be clouded by economic hardships stemming from Gamal's economic liberalization. Growing dissatisfaction with the consequences of economic reform would manifest itself publicly, and Islamists—capitalizing on new opportunities in a more open political system—will seek to mobilize the population in their favor. This Egyptian variant on "glasnost and perestroika" would increase instability rapidly and create the conditions for an Islamist seizure of power.

In the second, more likely scenario, the Gamal government's pursuit of economic reform would not be complemented by corresponding political liberalization. The Egyptian state would become increasingly repressive as it sought to control a population angered by the consequences of economic reform. Whether and for how long Gamal could control such discontent will determine the length of time before Islamists mobilize the Egyptian population in an attempt to seize power from the regime.

The most important task facing Gamal will be to manage the regime's relationship with the Islamists, who would seize the opportunity to convert their immense informal social strength into significant gains in the political sphere. Depending on the actual goals of the Islamists, such political gains may set the scene for conflict between Gamal's policies of political and economic reform and those of the Islamists. Although political reforms may appease the small minority of Egyptian intellectuals and liberals, the consequences of economic reform are likely to have a profound impact on the deep structures of Egyptian society.

Compounding the difficulty of economic reform, in Egypt, as in many other nations in the Middle East, governments do not engage in open and competitive bidding and procurement. *Bakshis* means not just bribery, but a system of favors that prevents a free market. This economic corruption reduces support for governments and restricts opportunity and employment. Such conditions contribute in some ways to the growth of jihadism. Governments would be well advised to have active inspectors general, ombudsmen, and offices of governmental accountability to ferret out such economic corruption. The surprised citizenry would be more favorably inclined toward their governments, at least for a short time.

In Egypt, a tango of economic reform and crisis has been playing out from the mid-1980s onward. During this period, economic reforms intended to improve the situation seemed only to yield a worsening social stratification. Riots and protests became a normal occurrence and even the repression of the state could do little to prevent uprisings. In 1991, there were twenty-six such events; in 1992, twenty-eight; and in 1993, sixty-three—all of them triggered primarily by the material losses of workers as a result of layoffs or the nonrenewal of contracts. The 1996 Human Development Report for Egypt indicates that between the years 1981 and 1991, poverty increased from 16.1 percent to 28.6 percent of the total population. Unemployment followed in the 1990s and rose from 8.6 percent in 1990 to 11.3 percent in 1996. Unofficial estimates of current unemployment in Egypt are as high as 20–25 percent of the population.

Discontent with Gamal's reform policies combined with the more open political system will result in increased protests, emboldening the

Islamists and promoting instability within the regime itself. It is likely that certain elements within Gamal's circle will find it beneficial to create links with the opposition as the political leverage of the Islamists increases. The Islamists, however, have yet to articulate how a distinctly Egyptian Islamic state would look. Indeed, the weakness of Islamists in Egypt lies in their inability to formulate a clear vision and program for the establishment of the Islamic state it seeks.

Most likely, Gamal's presidency will inaugurate an era of economic liberalism in Egypt. As for Gamal's intentions for reform on the political front, we can expect him to continue the repressive policies associated with his father's regime. In the short run, the continuance of authoritarianism will maintain a semblance of the stability in Egypt has demonstrated, on and off, for the past fifty years. Prospects for democratization, however, will fade. Increasingly repressive tactics will be needed to control opposition to Gamal's economic reforms. Gamal is likely to make minor cosmetic changes such as the sanction of new parties and increasing press freedoms so as to keep up the appearance of liberalization for Western audiences. The security services may become a less salient presence in daily life. More important, he will make no critical changes such as the banning of torture, an end to emergency laws, or amending the constitution. The Islamists will continue to be excluded from formal politics. Their enduring role in the informal sector, however, will allow them to capitalize on popular discontent more effectively than they have before. They will continue to offer subsidized education, food, and health care to a population that is increasingly unable to attain such primary goods from the state.

If these conditions were to spur renewed insurgency, along the lines of the low-level warfare of the 1980s and 1990s, the willingness of the armed forces to support Gamal will be a key factor in the way events unfold. Although the army leadership certainly sees its interests as inextricably bound up with the current and likely future political elite, the degree to which younger army officers have been Islamicized is unknown.

The Mubarak regime's approach to the challenges of an Islamist opposition has been complex and often contradictory. Ironically, the regime itself laid the foundation for Islamist mobilization of the population. The Egyptian state has sidelined the Muslim Brotherhood by excluding it from formal politics (although Muslim Brothers have been elected to legislative office under the label of other, sanctioned parties such as the Labor Party). In conjunction with this rejection of a role for political Islamist opposition, the Mubarak regime has assumed a deeper, more Islamic identity. To this end, the regime has given an esteemed role to conservative Azhari ulema within the education, media, and judicial sectors of government.

Thus, Egypt's Islamization can be partly traced to the Egyptian government's official support for Islam. Islam has also become the context in which conflicts between the state and the Islamist opposition takes place. This represents a relatively recent development that only began in the last twenty years. The state's own contribution to the Islamization of Egypt, therefore, has paved the way for increasing the popularity of the Islamists, who will always have a stronger Islamic social and political agenda than that of the government. This is a battle that the government can never win. Yet in maintaining its battle for political legitimacy in Islamic terms, the government will continue to strengthen the credibility and influence of the Islamist opposition and of Islamism as an ideology.

Jihadism is a latent force in Egyptian politics. This has been obscured since 1997, when Islamist groups in Egypt renounced violence and announced that they intended to work within the system for political change. The insurgency that plagued the Mubarak regime in the early 1990s dwindled away to the extent that some commentators have assumed that activist, violent extremism in Egypt is a thing of the past. Although it is true that outright jihadi violence has declined in Egypt, it is too early to assume that such violence has been brought to a complete halt. At this point, the Islamists claim to continue to work within the system for change. Given the fact that the system is rigged against them, this commitment cannot be guaranteed over the long term. Meanwhile, "jihadism" as an ideology of struggle continues to permeate the discourse and rhetoric of the opposition. As in Saudi Arabia, this jihad is framed as a struggle against the regime and foreign governments that support it, chiefly the United States.

The recent absence of religious violence in Egypt can be attributed not only to the Islamists' satisfaction in their gains at the grassroots level but also to the regime's effective use of the security services to clamp down on Islamists. Torture and arbitrary jailing continue to be mainstays of the Mubarak regime's war against Islamists, and it is this tendency—not any real decline in jihadism—that has marked an end to outright, visible violence. At the same time, government oppression of Islamists has played effectively into Islamist rhetoric on the regime's unrighteousness.

In this manner, human rights groups are often the first organizations to come to the support of Islamists, even though the groups' agendas are quite different.

The generational cleavages between older leaders of Islamist organizations and the younger, newer recruits may also have a significant impact on the Islamist movement. The younger cadres have been described as being less inspired by violent extremism than their forefathers, a majority of whom spent time in jail under Nasser, Sadat, or Mubarak. On the whole, however, it is too soon to conclude that the next generation of Islamists is relatively less extreme. Again, the early months of a Gamal Mubarak presidency may be extremely revealing on this point.

Anti-Americanism in Egypt is a vibrant force, in part because it has been encouraged by the government as a means of deflecting public attention from its shortcomings and, paradoxically, masking continuing cooperation with the United States. This is not to say that the public passively accepts such tactics, but in general, the overriding anti-American themes used by Mubarak's regime find a sympathetic audience. These themes include U.S. support for Israel, the plight of the Palestinians, and the status of morality in America, all of which continue to attract the attention of the public and intellectuals alike. Only 13 percent of Egyptians had a favorable opinion of the United States, according to the 2002 Zogby poll. Clearly, the regime benefits from coddling such discontent with the United States. The rise of Gamal Mubarak to office, however, may mark a gradual, if slight decline in the frequency and vehemence of state-sponsored anti-Americanism in Egypt owing to his commitment to increasing foreign investment. On balance, though, he is likely to walk the delicate line between the tactical deployment of anti-Americanism to buttress his domestic legitimacy in the media, while seeking to create strong ties between his administration and the American government.

IRAN

For nearly twenty years after the 1979 revolution, Iran enjoyed a relatively high level of internal stability resulting from its increasing international isolation, its embroilment in a series of military conflicts with its neighbors, and the general unpredictability associated with the new clergy-dominated rule of Ayatollah Khomeini. In large part, the stability of the system resulted from general agreement among those in power on the course, pace, and content of the revolution.

The 1997 election of reform-oriented Mohammad Khatami as president of Iran represented a second revolution of sorts in Iranian politics. This "second revolution" has largely failed to realize its goal of liberal democracy in a distinctly Islamic and Iranian context. Despite the criticism of disappointed reformers, Khatami has been hesitant to sanction anti-regime activism.

The reason perhaps for Iran's continued stability in the wake of Khatami's 1997 election lies in the stalemate between elites, with status quo–oriented interest groups on one side and reformers on the other. The structure of governance in Iran contributes to this stalemate. Although reformers play a role within the bureaucracy and educational institutions, conservative forces dominate the judiciary, military, police, and media. The structure of government constrains legislative power by conferring on the clerical elite the rights to block electoral candidates from competing and to invalidate legislation deemed counter to revolutionary Islamic standards.

Neither conservative nor reformist forces represent homogenous groups with cohesive ideologies or completely shared interests. This fragmentation has hobbled conservatives' ability to respond creatively to reformers' demands, while impeding reformers' capacity to agree on the tactics, speed, or desired outcome of their overall program. The stalemate between conservative and reformist forces will likely persist as domestic and international issues absorb Iran's attention in the coming years.

Stability and democratization in Iran will be largely influenced by a set of international challenges facing the country. Iran is different from Saudi Arabia and Egypt in that domestic change is not linked closely to international challenges in those countries. Challenges facing Iran include: the stability and nature of the new regime in neighboring Iraq, continued American pressure against Iran's nuclear program, the role of the conservative hard-liners in clinging to vehement anti-Americanism, and the general isolation of the Iranian regime from a population that is increasingly tied to the rest of the world through cultural, informational, and social interactions. The manner in which Iran responds to this series of "wild cards" will define the context in which democratization will advance or stagnate.

It is important to distinguish between two dimensions of Iranian society, namely, the citizenry and the regime. Within each group, further categorization separates clerics from lay people, liberals from conservatives, and radicals from reactionaries. In general, the two exist in a symbiotic relationship in which the regime requires the sanction of the people to maintain its revolutionary legitimacy, and the citizenry, in turn, look to the regime for reform and change. This distinction between state and society is crucial to accurately understanding the pursuit of democratization and the nature of anti-Americanism in Iran.

First, regional dynamics arising from American interventions in the Middle East factor in as a key determinant of Iran's stability. With American forces in both Iraq and Afghanistan, Iran will be forced to decide the nature of its relationship with the United States. Moreover, the possibility of the Khatami regime becoming an ally of the United States will also contribute to the importance of Iran determining its position vis-à-vis both the United States and a new Iraq. In this context, the traditional anti-Americanism of conservatives within the regime is an important factor. It is critical to distinguish between the regime and the population of Iran. Although conservatives who inveigh against the "Great Satan" dominate the regime, the population largely admires the United States. Iran stands apart in this respect in the region as one of the few states with a pro-American population in opposition to the anti-American sentiment of the government.

This duality of sentiment revealed itself most vividly in a recent poll conducted by the Ayandeh Institute. The September 2002 poll, commissioned by the Iranian Majlis' National Security Committee, found that 74 percent of Iranians favored resumption of relations with the United States and as many as 46 percent felt that U.S. policy toward Iran was "to some extent correct." Similarly, in 2003, in the shadow of the war in Iraq, an Iranian newspaper published a poll that was hosted on the web page of former Iranian president Hashemi Rafsanjani. In response to the question "What are the actual demands of the Iranian people?" as many as 45 percent chose "change in the political system, even with foreign intervention." Only 13 percent reflected the conservative hard-line view that the Iranian people demanded "the continuation of the present political policy."

Iranian regime-sponsored anti-Americanism differs from that of most Arab states in its revolutionary dimension. In many ways, anti-Americanism is a byproduct of the rhetoric of the 1979 revolution. The question remains as to whether such rhetoric plays any significant role at all in contemporary Iran. It is safe to say that attempts by the regime to deflect criticism through anti-Americanism are largely ineffective. Unlike in Saudi Arabia, anti-Americanism serves relatively little purpose within domestic politics.

Instead, anti-Americanism functions as a useful club that conservatives and reformers use to attack each other, but rarely use to increase their legitimacy in the eyes of the people. For conservatives, anti-Americanism legitimates the continuing political repression associated with the revolution. Anti-Americanism allows conservatives to argue that they are upholding the revolutionary tradition. Reformers, on the other hand, may spout pro-American rhetoric as a means of signaling their opposition to the regime without stating it explicitly. Indeed, when President Khatami called for engagement with the United States, Iranians interpreted the move as a symbol of his commitment to political reform. In this respect, Iranian politicians—conservative and reformist alike—use their sentiments about America as a proxy expression of their own positions vis-à-vis the regime and the revolution that brought it to power.

It is important to note that anti-Americanism does exist among Iranians. Experts have drawn attention to three particular strands of anti-Americanism that deserve attention in the coming years: Iranian nationalists dedicated to Iranian primacy in the region, the leftist adherents of Third World socialist ideology, and traditionalists who fear that engagement with the United States will negatively impact Iranian culture and social values. Ultimately, however, the more important question regarding anti-Americanism is whether it plays a role in influencing Iran's policies. Historically, anti-Americanism has become a more important force in Iranian society when the United States has given it something to be angry about.

International crises have historically brought Iranian society together. For instance, President Bush's recent reference to Iran as part of an "axis of evil" witnessed a unified response of Iranians—conservative, reformist, or otherwise—denouncing American designs. Recent international scrutiny of Iran's nuclear development program and the sense that America has done little to respond to Khatami's gestures for rapprochement are likely to increase the disillusionment of the population in spite of its immense fragmentation of ideology. Serious efforts for domestic reform are likely to take a backseat as Iranian society reacts to increasing international pressure.

Both the conservatives and reformists will remain at an impasse, in part because both sides tacitly agree that the ascendance of either party over the other could lead to instability. In the meantime, more of the clergy is shifting to the reform camp, as are the rank and file of the Iranian Revolutionary Guard Corps.

Change, however, is not likely in the near- to medium-term. Iran's consensus-driven and informal style of decisionmaking, the vested interests of the clerical and business elite—especially in the government-dominated economy—and the lingering influence of the revolutionary tradition will all slow the transformation of the impulse for economic liberalization and political accountability. Deadlock, punctuated by occasional incremental progress, will continue to characterize the country's political and economic performance.

On balance, democratic values and practices enjoy a relatively high position in Iranian society, in contrast to most of its Arab neighbors. Regular elections have been held, though they are sometimes followed by reactionary measures. The 1997 elections, for example, delivered a reformist to the presidency on an ideological platform that challenged the interests, ideology, and status quo of the ruling regime. The problem, however, came after the regime realized that the mood of the people was with reform. Elections were allowed to continue regularly and on schedule, but the 2000 parliamentary and 2001 presidential elections witnessed the activist intervention by the Council of Guardians to reject the suitability of countless reformist candidates. Surely, this reactionary intervention calls into question whether elections in Iran have been as democratic as some have claimed.

Many commentators have noted that Iranians today enjoy a higher level of liberty than they ever had under the shah or since the revolution, due in large part to the leadership of President Khatami. Open criticism of the regime is lightly tolerated, but certain criticisms, such as attacking the personhood of Khomeini or the Islamic Revolution itself, remain taboo.

The 2005 election is likely to repeat the regime's pattern of restricting the participation of reformist candidates in the election to a select few. Khatami himself is likely to continue to advance limited reform within the framework of the revolution. Even moderate conservatives will advocate reform only to the extent that the system established by them will remain intact. Such a delicate balancing on the part of conservatives will be necessary for them to maintain a semblance of legitimacy in the face of an increasingly discontented population.

The biggest challenge to democratization is the regime's isolation from the people. Instead of integrating democratization efforts into its platform, the conservative elements will seek a path of "controlled liberalization." This recalls the "controlled liberalization" schemes used by leaders like Sadat and Mubarak in Egypt. What states like Egypt have revealed is the lengthy period of time such systems can actually remain stable. The question remains whether in the Iranian case, the massive pressure for reform from the population will encourage Iranians to call out more forcefully for—and possibly even seize for themselves—real democratization.

Perhaps the most important variable in the critical issue of democratization and stability remains the role, power, and function of the supreme guardian (the head of the Council of Guardians). In a political structure that elevates the power of the supreme guardian above all others, it ultimately represents the most important factor in determining increased democratization or continued repression. It is likely that debates about democratization in Iran in the coming years will revolve around various conceptions of what the power of the supreme guardian should be in a society that is at once Islamic and republican.

PAKISTAN

Pakistan is on the precipice of political instability. A double suicide bombing in December 2003 narrowly missed killing the president, Pervez Musharraf. Subsequent attacks against other senior Pakistani officials also nearly succeeded. In March 2004, Ayman al-Zawahri fueled the fire of religious dissent by calling upon Pakistanis to overthrow the Musharraf government.

What little stability Pakistan has is owed to a historical alliance between the military and religious leaders, which bears some resemblance to the alliance between the ruling family and the clergy in Saudi Arabia. This implicit alliance between the ruling military and the sectarian party leaders and clergy has been a constant of Pakistani politics since its independence. The "military-mullah alliance" has now emerged as the key feature of the Musharraf government.[2]

The renewed prominence of the relationship stems from Musharraf's rivalry with the so-called democratic opposition in Pakistan, which has been excluded from political participation since the 1999 coup that ended the civilian rule of Nawaz Sharif. Musharraf's strategy is to rely on religious parties for political support and marginalize mainstream secular parties, while asserting that Pakistan remains a democracy. Musharraf harbors a deep conviction that these secular parties were feckless when in power and served primarily as a cover for feudal families that looted and mismanaged the country. Although his preference might be that army rule continue—particularly given his belief that the army is the only Pakistani institution untainted by corruption—Musharraf understands that the army itself needs the cover of broader political participation to exercise control with at least a veneer of legitimacy. The senior echelon of the army also sees the need for some distance between the army as an institution and its administrative role, if only to preserve its reputation for competence amid multiple policy failures, especially in the economic realm. Moreover, the support Musharraf needs from the international community would be vastly more difficult to obtain if Pakistan made no effort to mask the authoritarianism of its current government.

With regard to elections, a report by the Human Rights Commission of Pakistan states:

> The vast majority of voters fell in the category of "captive voters"—prisoners (voting inside prisons was claimed to be 100 percent), state and local bodies employees, factory workers (who were driven to the polling booths located within the factory premises in controlled batches). Voluntary turnout was very low.[3]

Put simply, "Musharraf's main objective is regime survival, not creation of a democratic, tolerant culture by eliminating extremism."[4]

Reliance on the religious parties to provide this cover carries its own costs. These parties, especially the Jamiat ul-Islami (JUI), have never done particularly well at the polls. Typical returns in the years before the ascension of military government were quite low, around 2 percent of ballots cast. Their dismal performance was not due so much to their ideological cast, which resonated with a religiously committed public, but rather to their inability to provide the essential services that a ruling party can deliver to constituents. The JUI might have been appealing in its dedication to a strict form of Islam, but it could not get potholes filled. The government's new reliance on the support of these parties has increased their political clout, which they have not hesitated to deploy.

At the same time, Musharraf has sought to improve Pakistan's reputation as a responsible international player. To accomplish this, he has sought to cut down on terrorist infiltration of Kashmir, to adopt a conciliatory stance toward India, and to provide concrete support for the war on terrorism. Here, Musharraf's international agenda has clashed with his domestic political priorities.

Al Qaeda and the ideology of jihad also continue to affect Pakistan's stability. Public opinion surveys show that Osama bin Laden is an enormously popular figure in Pakistan. His popularity is inversely proportional to that of the United States, which functions as an all-purpose symbol of protest in a relatively discontented society. Bin Laden's now fabled role in the war against the Soviets during the 1980s forms the narrative base of his popularity. American pursuit of bin Laden is emblematic, for many Pakistanis, of a larger war they believe the United States is waging against Muslims. His successful attacks against the United States in 2001 consolidated his image as a self-denying hero.

The ideology of jihad flowered in the 1980s as well. During that period, the war against the Soviets and later against Mohammad Najibullah, the Communist ruler installed in Kabul by Moscow, was consistently labeled as a jihad. As a result, *jihad* has come to mean physical warfare—as opposed to inner spiritual struggle—in the imaginations of many Pakistanis, and it is understood to be a fateful battle between Islam and the West.

These conditions have been nourished by the proliferation of madrassas, especially those that are affiliated with militant Islamic political parties, such as the JUI. Although even the best estimates are shaky, there are currently as many as 10,000 madrassas in Pakistan, which is a dramatic increase from the roughly 200 or so that existed at the time of Pakistan's formation. These schools are thought to enroll between 1 million to 1.7 million students, compared to an official enrollment of 1.9 million in government primary schools. Most analysts attribute the explosive growth of madrassas to the collapse of Pakistan's public school system in the mid-1980s to mid-1990s due to underinvestment and general neglect. Madrassas are clearly going to have a significant role in Pakistan's future.

Although the curricula in these schools necessarily emphasize Koranic studies and Islamic ritual and practice, not all accord the same prominence to jihad as a key element of Islamic identity. According to the International Crisis Group (ICG), the madrassas' "constrained worldview, lack of modern civic education and poverty make them a destabilizing factor in Pakistani society" and render the students "susceptible to romantic notions of sectarian and international jihad." Indeed, it is widely known that schools sponsored or subsidized by extremist parties have used the student bodies at these schools as a recruitment base for the jihad in Kashmir and, formerly, the jihad in Afghanistan.

Not enough is known about curricular matters to assess which schools are teaching what sort of material. Nor is it clear that all enrollees are in these schools as a matter of ideological commitment. Given the virtual absence of a government-run alternative in many areas of the country, and the fact that many madrassas include health care and room and board, a majority of parents probably find madrassa education to be highly desirable on purely practical grounds.

Hemmed in on one side by his reliance on religious parties to shore up his legitimacy, Musharraf is pressed on the other by a U.S. administration intent on destroying al Qaeda infrastructure in Pakistan and neighboring areas of Afghanistan. This objective cannot be achieved without Pakistan's cooperation; but cooperation with the United States will inevitably arouse the enmity of religious parties and their affiliated jihadists, on which Musharraf's government relies. If there had been any uncertainty on this score, back-to-back assassination attempts against Musharraf surely erased it.

The U.S. approach thus far has consisted entirely of threats and pleadings. Pakistan has been designated a major non-NATO ally, which gives it preferential access to some kinds of military equipment. Washington has also turned a blind eye to Pakistani nuclear physicist A. Q. Khan's transfer of nuclear technology to Iran, North Korea, and Libya. The Bush administration has also backed a five-year, $3-billion aid package for Pakistan.

Musharraf's ability to meet Washington's expectations, given the serious countervailing pressures he faces, is open to doubt. As a way of navigating the Scylla of domestic political demands and the Charybdis of American pressure, Musharraf has become a "minimal satisfier," in the words of one expert. Thus, he periodically offers the United States a midlevel or senior al Qaeda militant, while prohibiting the deployment of U.S. troops to Waziristan and ordering generally unconvincing sorties of Pakistani forces into that region. He has little flexibility, since the deployment of government soldiers into the autonomous areas could unite tribal chieftains against him. As these conflicting pressures mount, Pakistan is going to become an increasingly unstable place.

Iraq

In September 2004, three prestigious think tanks, including the Center for Strategic and International Studies, delivered the same verdict: The Bush strategy for winning the peace in Iraq has failed badly. Leaked reports from officials with the National Intelligence Council confirmed that in the very best case scenario, Iraq will have a shaky security environment and unstable government in the coming years. In the worst-case scenario, the national intelligence estimate predicted a civil war.

Little has been written on the impact the Iraq war has had on the terrorist threat facing the United States. It is a bitter irony that Iraq has turned into the very thing we went to war to prevent: a terrorist sanctuary with an al Qaeda and jihadist presence that far exceeds what was there during Saddam Hussein's reign. The Bush administration's decision to go after Saddam before al Qaeda had been crippled and Afghanistan had been stabilized has had many negative effects, with four in particular worth highlighting.

First, Iraq has no connection to the terror threat facing the United States, and Saddam's removal has done nothing to lesson the threat we face from al Qaeda and the jihadists. Perhaps the most vivid demonstration of this point is that a year and a half after Saddam's removal, the terror alert level in America remains unchanged and there is anticipation of a major al Qaeda attack within the next few months. The simple fact is that even if Iraq magically turned into a stable, secure democracy one day, the United States could suffer another 9/11-type attack the next day.

Some have argued that Iraq has expanded our security perimeter; that it is better to fight the terrorists in Iraq than here in United States. It would be a fabulous argument, if only it were true. It mistakenly assumes that the terrorists killing U.S. soldiers and civilians in Iraq are the same ones who would be trying to attack the United States. The jihadist operations in Iraq are being conducted by a deadly mix of Sunni extremist groups, such as Abu Mus'ab al-Zarqawi's Tawid wa Jihad, foreign fighters eager to conduct jihad against the Americans, remnants of Saddam's regime, and criminal elements. These are not the people who have been targeting America. Rather, America has been targeted by the original al Qaeda organization; that group is indeed a leader in the global jihadist movement, but it is a separate and distinct entity from the terrorist presence inside Iraq. Over a period of years, a stable, free, and democratic

Iraq may be a positive force for change in the Middle East, but our mistakes in Iraq and the attendant boost to the jihadist cause has put us at a serious disadvantage to ever make that happen within a useful time frame.

This leads to the second effect, that the failure to provide the most fundamental of requirements—safety and security—after Saddam's overthrow has turned Iraq into a strategic opportunity for the jihadists to harm the United States. The terrorists were able to establish a presence in many Iraqi cities and towns and form an alliance of convenience with the remnants of Saddam's government. Over the past eighteen months, they have established firm control over several cities in Iraq and, more important, brought violence to almost all parts of the country. The randomness of violence has further undercut support for the new Iraqi government and the United States. A new battlefield for jihad has been created, one that is far more "lucrative" than Afghanistan turned out to be. By successfully conducting regular car bombings and kidnappings, the jihadists are trying to convince Iraqis and the rest of the Muslim world that the United States can't be trusted, that its promises of democracy, freedom, and security are merely empty words.

Third, Iraq has had little effect on the behavior of the real state sponsors of terrorism. In the aftermath of Saddam's overthrow, some in Washington argued that Iraq would send an unmistakable message to Iran and Syria: Change your behavior, or you're next. In fact, the opposite has happened. Not only has Iran continued with its nuclear program, but our invasion of Iraq has done little to deter Syria and Iran from continuing to sponsor anti-Israeli terrorism. Their support for Hizbullah and the Palestinian rejectionist groups, who are killing Israelis, remains as strong as ever. Although the Syrian government has opposed jihadism for decades and cooperated against al Qaeda, it has only recently begun combined border patrols with U.S. forces in Iraq. It continues to sponsor Hizbullah's terrorism and has recently rejected UN Security Council resolutions calling for the withdrawal of Syrian forces from Lebanon. Our mistakes post-Saddam have also afforded Damascus and Tehran the opportunity to "bloody our nose in Iraq," quietly supporting the insurgency inside Iraq and encouraging Hizbullah operatives to do the same. The result is that Iraq's neighbors, particularly Iran, are well positioned to influence events inside Iraq to the detriment of U.S. interests.

Fourth, the continued unrest in Iraq will further delay any U.S. effort to create a new international coalition to confront Syria and Iran's terrorist activities. The international consensus to confront state sponsors of terrorism evaporated as a result of the Iraq war, a point not lost on Damascus and Tehran. As a result, they will do everything in their power to further bog down U.S. efforts in Iraq. Ironically enough, we have contributed to creating the breathing room Syria and Iran so desperately needed to avoid international action in response to their terrorist activities.

As the analysis by the Army War College's Strategic Studies Institute, written by Jeffrey Record, argues, the war in Iraq was a "strategic blunder of the first magnitude." Instead of energetically pursuing the priority of creating an ideological counterweight to al Qaeda, we invaded Iraq and gave bin Laden exactly what he needed: new propaganda to fuel the battle of ideas and a new front in which to train and attack the United States.

Despite all the missteps, faulty planning, and false assumptions that guided Iraqi postwar planning, there is a still an opportunity to succeed in Iraq. It will be more costly and take longer than it should have, but the requirement that we succeed has not changed.

The invasion of Iraq cost us many friends and allies. To have any chance of reversing the current trend in Iraq, the next administration must directly approach European governments to persuade them that assisting in Iraq is directly in their national interest.

We should go to NATO allies with specifics in mind. If we simply levy demands on the Europeans, as we have done in 2004, we will not gain additional support. We can rebuild credibility with our allies by addressing international concerns in areas that are near and dear to our European friends' hearts and directly benefit us.

The government should capitalize on current concern over high oil prices and U.S. dependency on foreign oil to propose a joint research endeavor with the Europeans to develop new technologies for alternative energy. This is a win-win proposal: The environment is prominent in Europeans' minds (particularly after the Kyoto snub), and they are more advanced in this field. This will also be a concrete step toward eliminating a major national security vulnerability.

Notwithstanding the Bush administration's claim that the war on terror cannot be fought as a "police effort," we should seek to expand cooperation in bringing terrorists to justice. Hunting terrorists down and eliminating them is important, but enforcing the rule of law is critical. We cannot afford the diplomatic or operational repercussions that result from a case like that in Germany, where the Moroccan Abdelghani Mzoudi, indicted on more than 100 counts of assisting the 9/11 terrorists, was acquitted of all charges because the Bush administration refused to provide the Germans with evidence deemed "too sensitive." The United States should propose bolstering the capacity of international legal institutions and treaties. The institutions themselves may have limited utility, but our commitment to them will win favor with our allies.

On the basis of the leverage gained from the actions above, we should enlist our allies in a fast-track program to train Iraqis to provide for their own security and bring in additional troops. In order to improve the dangerous situation in Iraq, we need to spend assistance funds now, and fast. By spending less than $1 billion of the $18 billion that Congress allocated for Iraqi reconstruction, we have lost crucial momentum that would have won support from ordinary Iraqis by creating jobs and improving the country's dilapidated infrastructure. We need to get funds flowing immediately into small, quick-impact projects focused in Najaf, Sadr City, Fallujah, and other hot zones. Large-infrastructure projects are important in the long run; however, smaller sums, spread to thousands of community-based projects, are the best hope we have to deflate the insurgency. Reconstruction funds should be diverted from U.S. contractors to Iraqi organizations and U.S. procurement rules altered to permit such a change.

The United States must mount a massive marketing operation, making it plain to Iraqis and others that the United States has no plans for, or interest in, a permanent base for U.S. forces in Iraq; that we have no designs on Iraqi territory or oil; and that we will no longer permit reconstruction money to support sweetheart deals in Iraq for contracts that exclude Iraqi firms.

We should work with our allies to establish a stabilization fund, administered by a U.S.-approved UN high commissioner (similar to successful operations in Bosnia) who will work with Iraq to assist its transition to stability and democracy. Finally, we should cease the counterproductive assaults on the so-called no go zones. Civilian casualties and infrastructure damage done by such elective urban combat will, in the long run, strengthen anti-Americanism.

5. Partnering with the Islamic World

To defeat the international jihadist movement, the United States must promote discussion in the Islamic world of values such as democracy, civil liberties, nonviolence, and protection of noncombatants. Traditional propaganda mechanisms and mediums, such as television and radio programs, will only constitute a small part of the solution. In fact, public diplomacy efforts spearheaded by the U.S. government will most likely be looked on with skepticism in the Islamic world. The most effective public diplomacy initiatives will be those led by nongovernmental organizations, governments other than that of the United States, and leaders in the Islamic world.

The U.S. government should take an active role in stimulating such groups, governments, and individuals to assume these tasks. Public diplomacy efforts will be successful only if they are matched by modifications to the U.S. foreign policies that affect issues most important to the Arab world: the Israeli-Palestinian conflict, U.S. support for repressive but Western-leaning regimes, and the conflict in Iraq. Although changes in U.S. policy in the Middle East will not alter the jihadists' view of the United States, particular adjustments in policy would have an effect on general public opinion in the Islamic world (the outermost of our concentric circles), which in turn will undermine the jihadists' base of support.

At the present time, it would be difficult to overstate the extent and depth of American unpopularity in the Arab world. In some ways, the United States has become a lightning rod for Arab criticisms and frustrations. For example, a Shibley Telhami poll administered by Zogby in February and March of 2003 found that large majorities in all five Arab countries surveyed held an unfavorable opinion of the United States.[1] In three countries; Jordan, Morocco, and Egypt, 80 percent or more reported holding unfavorable impressions of the United States. A Pew survey, also completed in the run-up to the war in Iraq, similarly reported widespread anti-Americanism in the Arab world as well as in Muslim countries more generally.

In the case of Lebanon and Jordan, where the same questions were asked in the summer of 2002 and again in March of 2003, a further erosion of U.S. popularity was registered over time.[2] Due to the lack of survey research in the Middle East prior to the mid- to late 1990s, it is difficult to put America's favorability ratings in fuller historical context. It is abundantly clear, however, that the United States engenders negative associations in most parts of the Middle East and North Africa, and its standing has fallen precipitously since the onset of the second Palestinian intifada in the fall of 2000.

The purpose of a public diplomacy campaign is to change a target audience's opinion concerning a particular issue or set of issues. Implicit in the premise of public diplomacy campaigns is the idea that given a well-crafted and precisely delivered message, the intended audience cannot help but be influenced over time. Because public opinion can be shaped, a failure to "win hearts and minds" can be attributable to a misreading of the demographics, sloppy implementation, or a poorly calibrated appeal. This logic is frequently applied to the U.S. inability to curb rising antipathy toward America in the Arab world. The consensus is that the United States simply does not understand its audience or, in the words of one commentator, fails to "take Arabs seriously."[3]

The concept of public diplomacy is best understood as a subset of the instruments of strategic influence.[4] Whereas strategic influence encompasses both coercion and persuasion, public diplomacy typically focuses on the latter. An advisory group convened at the behest of the U.S. Congress to study methods for improving the application of public diplomacy defined it as "the promotion of the national interest by informing, engaging, and influencing people around the world."[5] In short, it is the art of shaping how the United States is perceived abroad through the management of information and the representation of America in the public sphere.

Perhaps the most recognizable component of public diplomacy is foreign broadcasting, as exemplified by the Voice of America and Radio Free Europe services. Other high-profile efforts include the U.S. attempt to win over the Vietnamese public with its Chieu Hoi (Open Arms) campaign and its earlier efforts to use media outlets to promote denazification in postwar Germany.[6] Public diplomacy can also operate in the opposite direction, in the sense that rather than communicating through leaflets, radio transistors, or televisions, foreign nationals can be brought to the United States in the hope of promoting American culture and values through firsthand exposure. Public diplomacy campaigns extend to both receptive and hostile audiences, seeking to reinforce positive perceptions as well as win over adversaries. Replicating the successful use of information campaigns during the Cold War has generated much of the interest in reenergizing public diplomacy today.

Although there is certainly truth to the notion that U.S. outreach in the region has been hindered by an inability to comprehend the nuances of Arab identity, linguistics, history, and iconography, those concerns are less important than the much stronger connection between anti-American attitudes and American foreign policy. Simply put, the effects of U.S. military, political, and economic engagement in the Middle East are too dramatic to be easily recast by rhetorical campaigns. Public diplomacy has a role to play in shaping America's image abroad, but in the immediate context of Arab public opinion, its impact will remain at the margins.

Assertions that improved public diplomacy can take the edge off growing anti-Americanism vastly underestimate the skepticism and sophistication of audiences in the Middle East and North Africa. The narratives of al-Jazeera and al-Arabiya are currently defeating the U.S. government's public diplomacy efforts in the Middle East. Those efforts are being defeated not because the United States has ceded the debate or is inept at pitching the story, but because of U.S. interventions that often contradict the self-promoting rhetoric.[7] U.S. foreign policy is neither uniformly "for" or "against" Arab interests, but America's record on the Israeli-Palestinian conflict, as well as its historical support for Western-leaning regimes in the region despite their unpopular and repressive rule, has reinforced anti-Americanism in the Middle East.[8] In addition to what happens in the future in Iraq, American action on these fronts will determine the popular standing of the United States in the region.

REACHING OUT TO THE ARAB WORLD

In a little over two years, the United States has embarked on three major public diplomacy initiatives in the Arab world: Radio Sawa, al-Hurra, and al-Iraqiya (see Table 5.1, page 95). Each of these efforts was designed to raise America's favorability ratings. For example, Radio Sawa was a direct response to the failings of Voice of America, which was plagued with poor signal strength and unimaginative content. In contrast, Radio Sawa promised to appeal to a younger demographic with the use of popular music as the initial hook. Similarly, al-Hurra was conceived to be an antidote to the growing influence of pan-Arab satellite television, specifically al-Jazeera. Finally, al-Iraqiya was intended to fill the information void in Iraq in the aftermath of the war, allowing the United States to get out in front of rumors as well as to give the coalition a forum for promoting its successes.

To their credit, all three of these outlets have quickly achieved significant market share and at least a modicum of credibility among their listeners and viewers (see Figures 5.1 and 5.2, page 96). Polling data show that 74 percent of Iraqis watch al-Iraqiya on at least a weekly basis and 21 percent of those consider it "objective."[9] Al-Hurra, though not boasting ratings as high as al-Iraqiya's, still claims a respectable average adult viewership of 29 percent in a dozen urban areas surveyed in North Africa, the Levant, and the Gulf region. Just over half of its viewers rate its news coverage as "very reliable" or "somewhat reliable." Finally, Radio Sawa has staked out a weekly following of 38 percent of listeners polled in six Arab countries, including a high of 73 percent in Morocco. Remarkably, four of five listeners feel its news meets the same reliability criteria. Thus, on the basis of both market penetration and trust, these initiatives certainly appear successful at first glance.

Although these surveys communicate a relatively positive picture, there are a number of key remaining barriers. In the case of al-Iraqiya, a ban on satellite dishes during Saddam Hussein's rule, combined with the effects of sanctions and war, means much of Iraq is dependent on a very limited slate of terrestrial broadcasts. For most areas of the country, this implies a maximum of four channels: al-Iraqiya, al-Alam, al-Sharqiya, and in the vicinity of Basra and Baghdad, al-Hurra.[10] This state of affairs is further reinforced by sporadic censorship of the leading satellite networks, first by the Iraqi Governing Council and more recently by the Iraqi Interim Government.[11] Although 95 percent of Iraqis surveyed in an April 2004 CNN/*USA Today*/Gallup poll reported owning a working television set, one-third or fewer received satellite broadcasts such as al-Jazeera and al-Arabiya in their homes. In contrast, 84 percent affirmed receiving al-Iraqiya without difficulty. Given this dependence on al-Iraqiya, it should come as no surprise that the station has achieved significant market share. A lack of alternatives makes Iraqis a "captive audience," in both the figurative and literal senses of the term. In fact,

Table 5.1[12]
U.S. Sponsored Arabic-Language Broadcasting

Initiative	Launch Date	Project Description
Radio Sawa (Middle East Radio Network)	March 2002	An Arabic-language network that broadcasts music and news to a target audience of 15–29 year olds in the Middle East via a combination of FM, medium-wave, short-wave, digital audio satellite, and Internet transmission resources. Separate programming targets Iraq, Jordan, and the West Bank, the Persian Gulf, Egypt, and Morocco. All five streams share a differentiated music program; however, the news is similar on the four non-Iraq streams. Radio Sawa plays an even split of Western and Arab pop, interspersed with about 5 hours of news each 24 hour cycle.
Al-Hurra (Middle East Television Network)	February 2004	With a focus on attracting a broad audience in the Middle East, the al-Hurra satellite television channel provides news, current affairs, and entertainment programming on a 24 hours, 7 days a week, basis. In total, it reaches 22 countries in the Middle East and North Africa. Programming focuses on news and information, including news updates twice an hour, two one-hour newscasts each evening, and current affairs talk shows. The channel also broadcasts information or educational shows on subjects including health and fitness, entertainment, sports, and science and technology.
Al-Iraqiya (Iraqi Media Network)	May 2003	Part of the Iraqi Media Network (IMN), al-Iraqiya was initially set up by the Science Applications International Corporation (SAIC) at the behest of the Defense Department. Al-Iraqiya broadcasts primarily news and information programming as well as a limited slate of Egyptian entertainment television, sports, and recycled MBC coverage. Recently, Harris Corp., in partnership with LBCI and al Fawares, received a $96 million contract in improve al-Iraqiya and expand IMN's presence to encompass two national radio channels, two national television channels, and a national newspaper. Al-Iraqiya is available through terrestrial broadcast.

Figure 5.1
Al-Hurra: Viewership and Perceived Reliability of News[13]

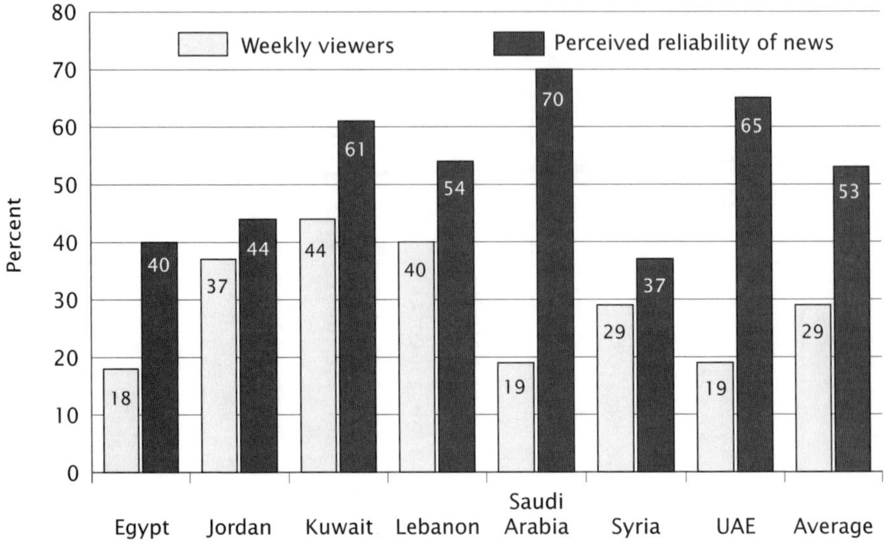

Figure 5.2
Radio Sawa: Listeners and Perceived Reliability of News[14]

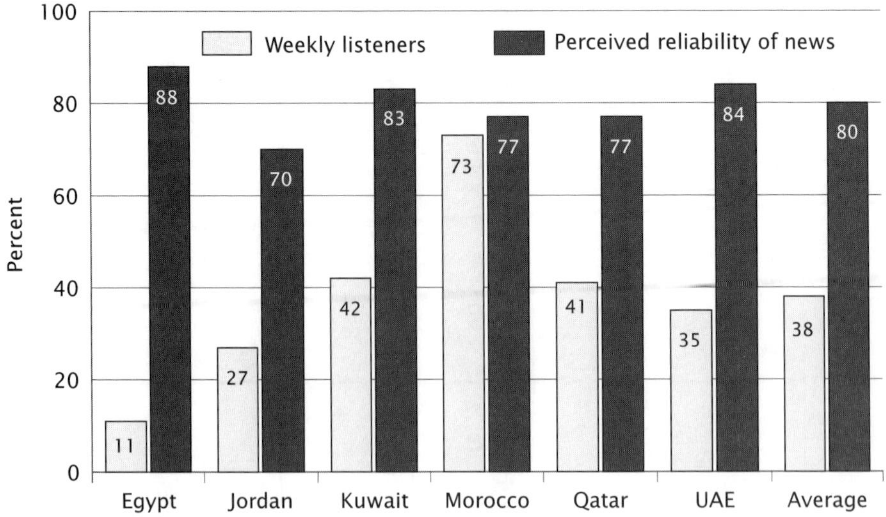

for those that do have a choice, a State Department–commissioned poll conducted in October 2003 found that 63 percent preferred al-Jazeera or al-Arabiya as a source of their news to just 12 percent for al-Iraqiya.[15]

On the other hand, al-Hurra's market share cannot be explained away as simply default television viewing. With the exception of Iraq, where the United States has taken steps to make al-Hurra accessible via terrestrial broadcast,[16] the station is available only to those households with satellite dishes. As such, time spent watching al-Hurra represents a choice over other free-to-air channels, including al-Jazeera, al-Arabiya, and so on. That said, given that the polling data presented in Figure 5.1 were compiled less than two months after its first broadcast, al-Hurra's ratings almost certainly reflect a bump due to its novelty. As the new player, and one whose launch generated a great deal of attention abroad, it makes sense that viewers would be curious to compare its content and formatting with other programming.

Because the figures include all respondents who acknowledged tuning in within the previous week, it is likely that most of those who responded positively were also supplementing their viewing with other news outlets. Thus, it is not possible to discern for what percentage of these viewers al-Hurra has supplanted pan-Arab or domestic media as their primary news source. Despite anecdotal reports that al-Hurra has been branded in the region as American propaganda, on balance those claims do not seem to be supported by the data.

Finally, with respect to Radio Sawa, there is a risk of overstating its influence by not accounting for the degree to which its listeners are self-selected. High-end estimates put its news coverage as a share of total programming at fifteen minutes of every hour.[17] Content is dominated by a mix of Arab and Western pop music designed to appeal to adolescents and young adults. This deliberate targeting of youth seems to be played out by Radio Sawa's actual following, given the fact that its weekly listenership within the fifteen-to-twenty-nine demographic is 69 percent higher than its share among the thirty-plus demographic.[18]

In addition to an audience that is heavily tilted toward a specific age structure, it is also self-selected on the basis of receptiveness to the United States (see Figure 5.3, page 98).[19]

On average, Radio Sawa listeners are more likely to be favorably inclined toward the United States vis-à-vis non-Radio Sawa listeners by a ratio of nearly two to one. Thus, in accounting for Radio Sawa's relative

Figure 5.3
Attitudes toward the United States among Radio Sawa Listeners and Nonlisteners[20]

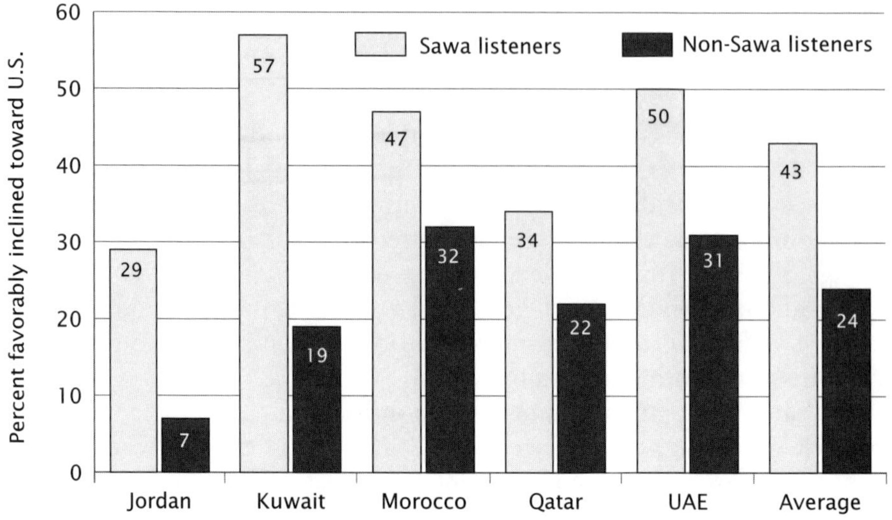

popularity, one must be careful not to conflate its appeal as entertainment value with more substantive influence. It would be a mistake (as well as condescending) to believe Arabs are not capable of drawing distinctions between American policies and popular culture. In the March 2003 Pew study, 42 percent of Jordanians and 57 percent of Moroccans reported liking American music, movies, and television, whereas 99 percent and 88 percent had unfavorable or very unfavorable opinions of the United States, respectively.[21]

THE BATTLE OF IDEAS

One of the enduring questions that has emerged from the debate over public diplomacy is why the United States has been so ineffective in associating itself with the values (principally freedom) enshrined in its founding. Some advocates recommend that the United States define itself as a symbol of freedom through broadcasting, exchange programs, outreach, development assistance, and so forth.

Following this logic, the proposed solution is more trained Arabists, more resources for public affairs, and more measurements to judge performance. These solutions, however, are based on the faulty premise that the careful management of perception will allow the United States to improve its image abroad while essentially bracketing foreign policy. This strategy may help at the margins, winning over a few fence-sitters and agnostics, but it is unlikely to turn the tide in any meaningful way. The United States could do a better job promoting interventions that have aided Muslims, such as the military campaigns and subsequent humanitarian efforts in Bosnia and Kosovo. And the United States should be urging the Arab world to reconcile the inconsistencies in Arabs' criticism of certain aspects of U.S. policy while failing to strongly condemn the behavior of Arab regimes in places like Darfur. Ultimately, these efforts are secondary to America's performance in Iraq, its role in mediating the Israeli-Palestinian conflict, and the character of its relationships with governments in the region.

In the March 2003 Telhami/Zogby poll, respondents were asked whether their "attitudes toward the United States are based more on your values as an Arab or on American foreign policy in the Middle East?" In each survey country, a plurality indicated that their opinion was influenced more by foreign policy considerations (see Figure 5.4, page 100). In short, these results confirm that much like the American public, Arabs care mostly about facts on the ground. There is nothing incongruous about life, liberty, and the pursuit of happiness and the values and aspirations of Arabs, but large majorities of those living in the Middle East and North Africa do evaluate U.S. foreign policy as out of step with their own worldview.

Of course, on no issue is the divide greater than with respect to the Israeli-Palestinian conflict. Not surprisingly, the Pew Center recently found that 96 percent of Palestinians, 94 percent of Moroccans, 77 percent of Kuwaitis, 99 percent of Jordanians, and 90 percent of Lebanese believe that U.S. policies in the Middle East "favor Israel too much."[22] Given the importance of this issue in the Arab world, there is little doubt that this fuels much of the animosity felt by Arabs toward the United States. Like all states in the international system, the United States must pursue policies based on self-interest, the special relationship with Israel included. However, realism also dictates that the United States internalize the cost of lost popular support in the region. Operating under the assumption that this can be offset or wished away through spin or smart campaigning is simply wishful thinking.

Figure 5.4
Basis for Attitude toward the U.S.[23]

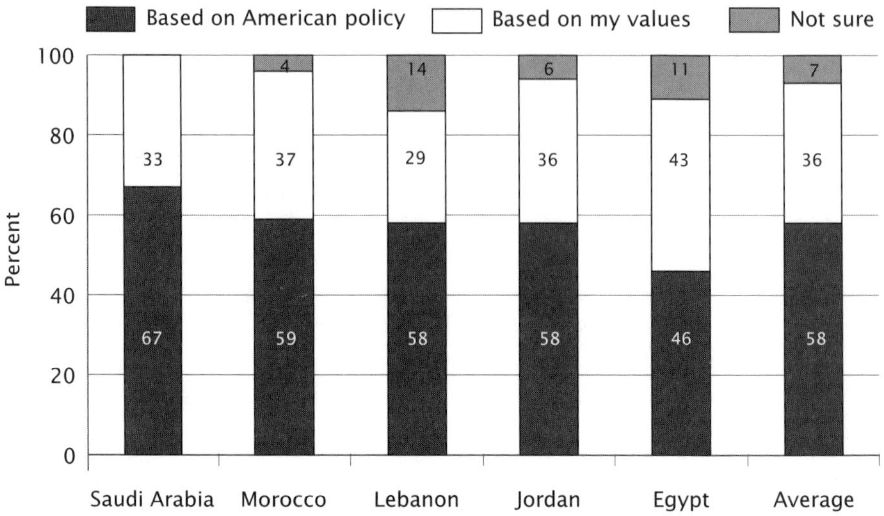

More important, an attempt to have it both ways is frequently counterproductive, leading to greater suspicion and prohibiting the United States from gaining any traction even when it is prepared to cede important points. This dynamic characterized the guarded reaction to President Bush's remarkable statements regarding "failed" U.S. Middle East policy in his November 2003 speech in the United Kingdom. Calling on the imperative of spreading freedom, Bush acknowledged, "We must shake off decades of failed policy in the Middle East. Your nation and mine, in the past, have been willing to make a bargain, to tolerate oppression for the sake of stability. Long-standing ties often led us to overlook the faults of local elites."[24] With the air already poisoned by Iraq and continued violence in Israel and Palestine, this mea culpa generated very little (if any) goodwill.[25] Simply put, U.S. action abroad sets the context for dialogue, and even significant shifts in rhetoric vis-à-vis the Middle East will remain a distant second to recorded votes (in the UN), the distribution of aid, and observable interventions. This is particularly true when those interventions are as momentous as regime change in Iraq and tend to reinforce the prevailing views of what really drives American foreign policy.

The United States needs to move beyond the model of public diplomacy employed during the Cold War. Instead of treating public diplomacy as a lever of influence, it may be time for the United States to lower its expectations and consider that approach to be a more modest element of a process of dialogue—not an instrument or a means to an end, but an end in itself. Given the trajectory of America's standing in the Arab world, this alone could be considered progress. Additionally, being more choosy in its appeals and working to divorce day-to-day information flow from policy objectives will ultimately help restore the credibility of the message. Until the United States reaches that point, overloading the airwaves cannot hope to produce the desired effect.

SUPPORT FROM MUSLIM GOVERNMENTS

The ability of Muslim governments to help the United States win greater understanding for its policies and objectives is limited by their own lack of credibility. Decades of controlled press reporting, government-owned broadcasting—which did little beyond televising footage from government meetings—and extravagant lies have undercut public trust. Mamoun Fandy has argued that trust in Arab Muslim societies derives from confidence in the "chain of transmission." In much the same way, Muslim scholars have assessed the reliability of traditions about the Prophet on the basis of isnad, the intergenerational record of the eminences who relayed these stories to one another over the course of centuries. In this chain of transmission, people whom one knows personally are to be trusted; impersonal institutions, such as a government repeatedly caught in lies, has no place in the chain. The problem is that the trustworthiness of a person who passes a story on to his friend may far exceed the trustworthiness of the material he passes on. Thus, outlandish stories about the United States might be perceived to be more credible if heard from a trusted source than more commonsensical accounts emanating from governments or media outlets perceived to be in league with, or controlled by, governments.

A related barrier to trust has been erected by Osama bin Laden and his spokesmen, who have argued that impious Muslims and infidels have constructed a vast edifice of lies intended to conceal the true nature of reality from honest Muslims. The implicit claim is that any assertion by the United States or its Muslim puppets is necessarily false. The truth can be inferred as the opposite of whatever the United States says. As an example, when the United States elected to support the road map for Israeli-Palestinian peace, bin Laden denounced it as a sly maneuver that was actually intended to enslave Palestinians. Similarly, Western intervention on behalf of Muslims in the Balkans has been dismissed as a ruse to further the denigration of Muslims.

Another impediment to a U.S. partnership with local governments in an effort to foster dialogue and improve America's image lies within these governments themselves. The Egyptian and Saudi governments, for example, not only permit but deliberately echo and reinforce anti-American themes in a bid to buttress their popular legitimacy. This policy, generally defended in a disingenuous way as respect for free expression, is a key element of their strategy for clinging to power while avoiding serious reforms. We therefore need to bear in mind, as we contemplate ways to enlist these governments in a campaign to improve Muslim understanding of the United States, that we will in effect be asking them to undercut their own perceived interests.

Nevertheless, several short- and long-term initiatives are worth considering. Among the short-term steps would be greater accuracy in official statements about issues involving the United States. In particular, governments in the region could contribute to a better public understanding of American motives by avoiding gross mischaracterizations of American actions and their consequences. This does not require that governments concur in U.S. policy or publicly support it. But it does mean that members of the political elite, including heads of government, refrain from saying, for example, that the United States has perpetrated massacres or is engaged in Iraq for reasons of conquest and enrichment. Given the linkage between the United States and Israel that many in the region take for granted, leaders should take care to cast their statements on the Palestinian-Israeli conflict in a way that does not exaggerate the level of violence, addresses the issue of blame in a more evenhanded way, and acknowledges the history of U.S. efforts to bring the parties to a settlement.

Senior members of the Egyptian government, for example, concede that Arafat's leadership has impeded the Palestinian ability to capitalize on Israeli concessions and win American support. Yet these officials would never make such statements to their own publics. All governments engage in a form of diglossia—speaking in one "language" to domestic audiences and in another to foreign interlocutors. We should not expect foreign governments to be purer than our own in this respect. Yet a greater convergence between the rather more sophisticated views they express in private and the statements they make in public would be constructive.

Medium-term measures might include government help in countering the baneful exuberance of the media regarding the United States. Washington cannot, of course, encourage censorship. But foreign leaders can directly challenge the more pernicious claims that appear frequently in regional media regarding U.S. aims and objectives in the region. Elites can take a strongly vocal stance toward anti-Semitic stories that not only demonize Israel but, more important, purport that the United States is under the control of Jews and seeks to advance Jewish interests. Governments that are themselves suspected by their publics of participation in American plans for domination of the region will not persuade many that grand conspiracy theories are wrong. Nonetheless, they will convince some; and it is essential that these often bizarre stories be challenged in Arabic by Arabs. Government silence constitutes implicit concurrence in these myths and enhances their power.

Although the appearance of such stories and the prevalence of inaccurate reporting are due as much to editorial agendas as to low standards among reporters, government funding for journalism training would improve the quality of reporting over time.

One of the obstacles to better intercultural comprehension is a set of deeply embedded, negative beliefs about the United States. Ian Buruma and Avishai Margalit have called these formulaic notions "Occidentalism," in homage to the late Edward Said, who had earlier dissected a reciprocal set of ideas about the Arab world that pervaded Western scholarship for many years—"Orientalism." Occidentalist views hold that the United States is a soulless place enslaved to technology, where money is all-important, morals are low or nonexistent, pornography and degradation of women are ubiquitous, and violence permeates society and governs foreign policy. Sayyid Qutb, the Salafi thinker executed by the Egyptian government in 1965, wrote the classic statement of this view upon his return from a year in the United States.

Like all stereotypes, there is a grain of truth in these images; taken as a whole, however, they are highly misleading and open the door to misunderstanding of specific actions or statements by the United States about matters that concern Muslims generally and Arabs in particular. Governments might help counter these Occidentalist beliefs by enriching public discussion of American history and culture. Toward this end, governments could subsidize or otherwise encourage documentaries about the United States and sponsor in-depth reporting about American life and history that reveals the flaws in common stereotypes about America. This could not be expected to rapidly reverse resentments against the United States, if only because there are aspects to American life and society that resemble the stereotype. It would, however, engender a sense of the complexity of American life and perhaps—over time—erode the widespread impression that our society is fundamentally alien.

Another significant obstacle to better understanding lies in the power of the pulpit. Clerical preaching about the United States has become more negative over the past decade. This is true not only in the Middle East but in other countries where there are a large number of Muslims, including Nigeria, Indonesia, Russia, the United Kingdom, and Pakistan. Religious language is a powerful conveyor of values and ideas. As a result, preaching that demonizes the United States, portraying it as singularly opposed to Islam, and perpetuating Occidentalist perceptions of American society, can do much to damage the position of the United States.

In many Middle Eastern countries, there are limits to what clerics can say overtly. Scriptural language, however, offers numberless "coded" ways to refer to the United States, without referring explicitly to the United States or its actions. Moreover, the mosque is not the only platform for anti-American preaching. Star-quality clerics are recorded for wide dissemination via audiotape, and their cassettes are available in markets all over the region. Preachers who take a more moderate line are often thought of as "ulema as-Sulta"—essentially government parrots—and therefore disregarded. Against this background, options open to governments are obviously limited. Despite these constraints, governments could indirectly sponsor moderate clerics who believe in the compatibility of Islam with Western values and stress Islam's nonviolent dimension. The difficult pieces of this stratagem are the scarcity of clerics who hold these views, the chilling effect of radical preachers on those who do hold moderate views, and the relative obscurity and generally low-wattage delivery of moderate sheikhs. (Safar al-Hawali, a fiery Saudi preacher who has been "turned" by the Saudi government, is a useful counterexample.) These constraints, however, are not necessarily fatal. The United States and its foreign partners might usefully discuss the feasibility of efforts to shape clerical discourse in a way that fosters greater understanding of the United States.

Over the long term, the best thing Arab governments can do is improve their educational systems and reform outdated curricula. Spending is not the problem; budgets for education as a share of government spending are extraordinarily high throughout the region. But poorly educated teachers, instructional methods that do not foster critical thinking, and obsolete curricular materials are common problems. In countries where the Saudi *tawhid* curriculum has been established, suspicion of non-Muslims and disregard for their religious beliefs are curricular objectives. Unless and until these shortcomings are remedied, American expectations of a more informed discourse about the United States—and a greater willingness to consider its side of the story—are unlikely to be met.

Finally, there is the issue of context. In recent years, American actions and self-expression have reinforced many of the pernicious beliefs that the United States wishes to counteract. Unless Americans give greater thought to the effect of their actions on the views of others, a focus on what foreign governments can do to reverse negative views of the United States will prove unavailing.

In order to win the "Battle of Ideas," the United States must leverage the power and attractiveness of common values that we share with the Islamic world. In the wake of Abu Ghraib, we must work even harder to overcome misunderstandings and the propaganda that terrorists use to expand their spheres of influence. Together with the Europeans, we must engage in a concerted program to fight religious intolerance against Islam, at home and abroad. These efforts must support human rights agendas and strengthen educational systems and economic opportunities, especially for women.

In addition to countering the jihadist terrorists with law enforcement, intelligence, and military measures, we must erode support for them in the Islamic world through what the 9/11 Commission called the "Battle of Ideas." Nations other than the United States (including both Islamic and non-Islamic countries) and nongovernmental organizations must take the lead in active programs to appeal to Muslims to denounce intolerance and terrorist violence done in the name of Islam. These efforts must stress our common values and overcome misunderstandings and terrorist propaganda. Reactivating the Israel-Palestine peace process must be a part of this larger effort.

As part of the Battle of Ideas, the United States and Europe must demonstrably welcome Islam as a part of their cultures. For Europe, that means both fighting anti-Islamic discrimination in European Union countries and initiating discussions on Turkey's accession to the European Union.

Turkey is an Islamic democracy, with a free press and equal rights for women. It allows religious freedom and combats the jihadists. Yet Turkey's long-term stability and its ability to resist jihadist forces is dependent upon its economic health. That health is, in turn, almost certainly dependent upon its admission to the European Union. Turkey can be a model and a partner for other Islamic nations, or it can devolve into the kind of chaos that we have witnessed in Pakistan and Algeria. The difference depends upon whether the EU nations can overcome their own racism and prejudices, whether they will insist that the EU is a "Christian" entity. Thus, for both the European Union and the United States, winning the Battle of Ideas means a concerted program to fight religious intolerance against Islam on every front.

Although jihadist terrorists are often not poor or uneducated, they use the underprivileged populations in some Islamic nations as one base for their support and as a lever for undermining national stability. The United States, the European Union, and the international financial institutions must greatly expand their financial and programmatic support for development efforts in Afghanistan, Uzbekistan, Pakistan, Yemen, Jordan, Morocco, and other economically challenged Islamic nations. These efforts must support human rights efforts and strengthen educational systems and economic opportunities, especially for women.

6. Going after the Jihadists

In addition to working to erode support for the jihadist terrorists, we must undertake actions using our law enforcement, intelligence, military, and financial capabilities to eliminate those terrorists and their organizations. This chapter outlines strategies that we should pursue in each of those four areas.

Law Enforcement
Increasing Capabilities While Protecting Civil Liberties

The FBI is the leading U.S. counterterrorism law enforcement organization. Prior to 9/11, the FBI proved to be incompetent in pursuing al Qaeda in the United States but contributed significantly to investigatory activities abroad. Since 9/11, the FBI has slowly improved its domestic capabilities. But it still lacks sufficiently trained analysts and effective technology. Rather than creating a new domestic intelligence agency, it is best in the near term to create a new "agency within the bureau"—a completely different kind of organization—as a component of the FBI. This new unit must have its own budget, personnel, and procurement systems, and a different bureaucratic culture. To achieve the needed technological modernization, significant support functions should be completely outsourced with special incentive contracting. Within the new unit, analysts must be given priority over agents, and prevention over arrests. The new unit must develop sources and engage in agent penetrations of potential threat groups, as the FBI has done in the past with the Cosa Nostra and the Ku Klux Klan.

The "agency within the bureau" must be supported by police intelligence units in major metropolitan areas. These intelligence units should be subject to oversight by an office within the U.S. Department of Justice to help avoid civil liberties abuses. Similarly, the 9/11 Commission's recommendation of an independent, outside, civil liberties oversight board should be adopted. The recently created civil liberties panel consists exclusively of federal bureaucrats and is advisory, rather than performing an oversight role. It cannot be relied upon to prevent excessive incursions on civil liberties.

INTELLIGENCE

The 9/11 Commission's recommendations, and the subsequent detailed proposal by Senate Intelligence Committee Chairman Pat Roberts (R–Kansas), form a basis for reform of the U.S. intelligence community to more effectively fight jihadist terrorism. The key elements of these proposals are:

- One senior official should be accountable for all U.S. intelligence agencies.
- That senior official should have budgetary and personnel authority, not merely coordinating responsibilities.
- Control of the National Security Agency, National Reconnaissance Office, and National Geospatial Intelligence Agency should be shifted from the Defense Department to the national intelligence director.
- The new national intelligence director should direct the FBI's domestic intelligence agency.
- The current analytical unit within the CIA (the Division of Intelligence) should be renamed the Office of National Assessments and should be an independent agency, separated from the intelligence collection agencies.
- A separate human intelligence agency, on an equal standing with the other intelligence collection agencies, should be created from the CIA's current Directorate of Operations.

- An organization should be created dedicated to the exploitation of unclassified, public information—known as "open source" intelligence.

All of these proposals are workable, justified, and essential to intelligence reform. None of them would diminish the ability of intelligence agencies to support the needs of the "war fighter" in peacetime or during conflicts.

The separation of the analytical function from the human intelligence collection agency is key to the independence of the evaluation and assessment functions. Keeping analysts and human intelligence collection officers together has proven in the past to distort evaluations and make it difficult for the analysts to be critical of the shortcomings of the "spy" agency.

The "spy" capabilities of the Central Intelligence Agency (CIA) have been judged to be inadequate by the outgoing and incoming CIA directors, both of whom have suggested that it will take at least five more years to achieve an adequate capability. Much of the inadequacy stems from the overreliance on agents posing as diplomats and the shortage of "not official cover," or NOC agents. Former agent Reuel Gerecht has proposed limited-term contract NOC agents (rather than career agents) compensated at much higher salaries ($250,000, compared with current rates of about $80,000) in order to recruit high-quality agents, who must live overseas for years without contact with their American families.

Much of the CIA's failures to deal with al Qaeda in the 1990s stemmed from an institutional reluctance to engage in operations that risked personnel or the reputation of the agency. Both the president and the congressional oversight committees must make clear their desire that the intelligence agencies be less risk averse. They must be willing to accept failures and casualties.

The Military

The U.S. military performed brilliantly in Operation Enduring Freedom and Operation Iraqi Freedom. Both campaigns saw the debut of new technology and new tactics that paid immediate benefits. One key component of those missions was the greater use of special operations forces (SOF) in all levels of combat. Gone were the days when SOF was relegated to SCUD hunting or reconnaissance missions. In Afghanistan and Iraq, we witnessed an unleashing of SOF capability that provided an overwhelming advantage for the United States to win battles quickly and decisively.

But we are unlikely to see another large-scale military operation in the name of counterterrorism for the foreseeable future. The continued problems in Iraq and the force presence requirements there will severely hinder America's ability to conduct major operations against Iran or other state sponsors of terrorism. As a result, emphasis will shift to operations against non-nation-state targets, such as terrorist leadership and terrorist training camps, in both permissive and nonpermissive environments. This potentially means operations in nations such as Pakistan, Uzbekistan, Yemen, the Philippines, and Indonesia, as well as parts of Africa. Such missions will place a premium on SOF that are agile, independent, and fully equipped.

One of the major successes of the Afghanistan and Iraq campaigns was the use of the Predator Unmanned Aerial Vehicle (UAV). The Predator provided outstanding real-time intelligence to military forces and was able to conduct its own strike missions when armed with the Hellfire missile. This capability should be a cornerstone for future special operations counterterrorism missions. U.S. Special Operations Command (SOCOM) should be provided with a dedicated Predator UAV capability, for both reconnaissance and strike missions, and sufficient infrastructure so it can be deployed globally.

While Secretary of Defense Donald Rumsfeld and Deputy Secretary Paul Wolfowitz have extolled the performance of SOF in the Global War on Terrorism, they have not backed up their words with appropriate resource support. SOCOM remains understaffed and underresourced. A major priority in the next administration must be to provide SOCOM with the resources necessary to become a lead player in military counterterrorism operations. Moreover, the centrality of SOCOM's role means it must also become a truly "supported" command center in which the regional "CINCdoms," such as Central Command (CENTCOM) and Pacific Command (PACOM), provide manpower and assets to missions where SOCOM is the lead. This process began with the Pentagon's fiscal year 2004 budget; but it must be accelerated and broadened.

Another major innovation, especially in Afghanistan, is the cooperation between the CIA and SOF in prosecuting terrorism targets.

Sustaining and expanding this cooperation will be critical for success in both the permissive and nonpermissive environments in which the U.S. military will be working. This means more effective integration between SOF and the CIA Clandestine Service. To ensure a better understanding of the respective capabilities of SOCOM and the CIA and a dismantling of the bureaucratic and cultural barriers that hinder more effective joint operations, they should conduct more joint training, education, and exercises.

Even though stronger cooperation between the CIA and Defense Department is necessary, the military should not have to rely on the CIA's covert operatives to support military operations. In the past, this has made SOF too dependent on the CIA's bureaucracy. A proper SOF capability means the military must have its own cadre of covert operatives. This would be done through reconstitution of the military not official cover (NOC) program, which will give the special operations community a valuable asset to support its operations on a global basis. Special Forces must be expanded and must be encouraged to conduct small unit, covert anti-terrorist operations when local governments will not act. Such operations may result in U.S. casualties. Congress and the White House must make clear in advance that they understand and accept the casualty risks.

Terrorist Financing

As long as al Qaeda maintains a lucrative financial network, it remains a lethal threat to the United States. And al Qaeda still has money to fund terrorist operations. The financial network that currently supports al Qaeda is diverse and ever-changing, taking advantage of unprotected or undetected opportunities to raise, hold, and move funds. Yet there is a central "theory of the case" that characterizes U.S. understanding of the al Qaeda financial network and guides U.S. actions to disrupt it and track it back to specific terrorist cells and leaders.

The 9/11 Commission concluded that before the 2001 attacks, al Qaeda received about $30 million per year. This sizable fund was not simply the wallet of just one man, Osama Bin Laden, no matter how rich he once was. If that were the case, it would be a much easier problem to address.

Instead, al Qaeda obtained money continuously from a variety of sources. Money was—and is—raised through Islamic charities and notable financial facilitators, and also through legitimate businesses and criminal enterprises. It is moved through formal banking channels; less formal alternative remittance systems, such as the centuries-old *hawala* network; and the very oldest method—bulk cash couriers and other smugglers. More recently, al Qaeda and its affiliates appear to be relying more on other methods to support their operations. Funding for the cell responsible for the Madrid bombings earlier this year, for example, appears to have depended on common criminal activity and drug trafficking.

The best publicly available descriptions of the al Qaeda financial network can be found in two publications of the 9/11 Commission—its report and its subsequent "Monograph on Terrorist Financing"—and in the 2002 and 2004 reports of the Council on Foreign Relations Independent Task Force on Terrorist Financing, which anticipated many of the findings and recommendations of the 9/11 Commission.

For years, U.S. policymakers were poorly served by weaknesses in their intelligence on al Qaeda's finances. As the 9/11 Commission's monograph accurately described, "even after the September 11 attacks, the intelligence community could not estimate the total income or the relative importance of any source of bin Laden's revenue stream" and even to this day "the U.S. government still has not determined with any precision how much al Qaeda raises or from whom, or how it spends its money."

The CIA had "incomplete understanding of al Qaeda's methods to raise, move, and store money, and thus hampered the effectiveness of the overall counterterrorism strategy." And the FBI "did not systematically gather and analyze the information its agents developed" and "as an organization failed to understand the nature and extent of the problem or to develop a coherent strategy for confronting it." Before 9/11, the CIA was trying, but failing. The FBI wasn't even trying.

THE PARTICULAR PROBLEM OF SAUDI ARABIA

Still, what we knew then—and know now—about this financial network showed that it is global in its reach, including into the United States. Yet historically, individuals and organizations based in the Gulf region have been the single most important source of funds for al Qaeda, as well as other terrorist groups such as Hamas.

As the 9/11 Commission concluded in its final report this year: "Al Qaeda appears to have relied on a core group of financial facilitators who raised money from a variety of donors and other fund-raisers, primarily in the Gulf countries and particularly in Saudi Arabia." And back in 2002, a Council on Foreign Relations task force concluded that "for years, individuals and charities based in Saudi Arabia have been the most important source of funds for al-Qaeda; and for years, Saudi officials have turned a blind eye to this problem."

Has the Saudi Arabian government itself funded terrorism? Perhaps to "pay off" al Qaeda to prevent domestic attacks, knowing that the regime itself is the group's primary target? These allegations have been made for years, but no convincing evidence has yet emerged. However, widespread interest in searching for a "sin of commission" tends to obscure the Saudis' glaring "sin of omission"—their astounding negligence. As the 9/11 Commission's monograph found regarding Saudi Arabia, "a lack of awareness of the problem and a failure to conduct oversight over institutions created an environment in which such activity has flourished."

Before the 2001 attacks in the United States, Saudi Arabia resisted any real cooperation with the United States on terrorist financing. And even later, as the 9/11 Commission's monograph aptly described, "from the 9/11 attacks through spring 2003, most U.S. officials viewed Saudi cooperation on terrorist financing as ambivalent and selective"—all this while the president, his spokesperson, and a chorus of his top advisers publicly expressed their satisfaction with Saudi efforts. Only after al Qaeda bombed targets within the kingdom in May and November 2003 did the Saudis finally focus on the problem and improve their cooperation with the United States.

At its core, efforts to combat terrorist fund-raising also require a successful "war of ideas" to denounce and discredit the ideology that attracts foot soldiers, supporters, and potential donors. Here, too, Saudi Arabia is a central front, as the government and Saudi-based organizations spend huge amounts of money supporting madrassas, Islamic centers, and mosques around the world that all spread a particularly intolerant and anti-Western version of Islam.

The bottom line, as the 9/11 Commission Report noted, is that "Saudi Arabia has been a problematic ally in combating Islamic extremism."

WHAT HAS BEEN DONE

Immediately after 9/11, the United States took a number of actions to combat terrorist financing, including a prominent series of "blocking actions" against suspected terrorist assets. These tend to capture only a small amount of actual funds but are very useful in "encouraging" other countries to take their own actions against suspected terrorist financing elements. The issue became prominent in U.S. diplomacy, international law enforcement, and intelligence activities. The United States also worked through multilateral organizations like the Financial Action Task Force to build a global consensus on the oversight of charities, among other issues. And at home, despite Republican opposition, Congress added anti–money laundering provisions to the Patriot Act.

Momentum slowed notably only months later, however, as the Bush administration put this issue on the proverbial "back burner," calling on a subcabinet official at the Treasury to coordinate interagency efforts and publicly announcing a "second phase" in the effort that would be characterized by fewer public designations of terrorist financiers. As preparations for the war on Iraq took center stage, the heat was turned down on Saudi Arabia. An implicit arrangement allowed the United States to continue to impose "blocking actions" against Saudi persons and institutions, but only in the context of a "joint" designation with Saudi Arabia. As the 9/11 Commission's monograph put it, during this period "U.S. efforts to overcome Saudi recalcitrance suffered from our failure to develop a strategy to counter Saudi terrorist financing, present our requests through a single high-level interlocutor, and obtain and release to the Saudis actionable intelligence."

However, in response to the May 2003 terrorist attacks, Saudi officials started to address the mindset that enables and condones acts of terrorism. These measures have included steps toward educational reform and limited measures intended to discipline (or "reeducate") certain extremist Islamic clerics—at least those operating in Saudi Arabia. There has been less decisive action taken to curb the billions of dollars funding the extremism abroad.

Saudi Arabia has taken important actions to disable domestic al Qaeda cells and has increased its tactical law enforcement and intelligence cooperation with the United States. Interior Ministry and other Saudi law enforcement and intelligence officials are now regularly killing al Qaeda members and sympathizers in violent confrontations. Saudi

Arabia has also largely improved its legal and regulatory regime. Since 9/11—and particularly since the May 2003 Riyadh bombings—Saudi Arabia has announced the enactment or promulgation of a plethora of new laws and regulations and the creation of new institutional arrangements to combat money laundering and terrorist financing.

But Saudi Arabia has not fully implemented its new laws and regulations. The first step toward the creation of an effective anti–money laundering and counterterrorism financing (AML/CTF) regime is the passage of laws and regulations—but that is just the first step. Just as important—and more important over the longer term—is effective implementation and execution of these laws. Some aspects of that effort, such as comprehensive compliance with record-keeping provisions, may take time. But other aspects of implementation, such as standing up and funding new organizations and oversight bodies, can be accomplished more readily.

Additionally, Saudi enforcement actions directed against al Qaeda have largely avoided financiers. There is no evidence that since 9/11, Saudi Arabia has taken public punitive actions against any individual for financing terror. Although Saudi Arabia says that it has taken nonpublic actions against financiers, responses taken in the shadows may have little consistent or systemic impact on ingrained social or cultural practices that directly or indirectly threaten the security of the United States.

The Bush administration remains unusually and unconstructively reluctant to criticize Saudi Arabia on this subject. President Bush even remained silent when the Saudi crown prince publicly announced that Israel, not al Qaeda, was responsible for the bombings in his country.

THE WAY FORWARD

The U.S. government is still not organized properly to combat terrorist financing at home or abroad. For several years after 9/11, the general counsel of the Treasury Department led the Bush administration's efforts. Even the most competent Treasury general counsel is poorly equipped, from an institutional standpoint, to lead such important work. This is a job for the White House. Therefore, the president will first need to take steps that relate to the organization and operations of the U.S. government. He should then build a fundamentally new framework for U.S. relations with Saudi Arabia. Finally, he should also build a structure that will force the U.S. government to take a hard look on an enduring basis at the level of cooperation from all countries, not just Saudi Arabia, with U.S. efforts to curtail the financing of terrorism.

The next president should designate a special assistant to the president for combating terrorist financing at the National Security Council with the specific mandate to lead U.S. efforts on terrorist financing issues. Such an official would direct, coordinate, and reaffirm the domestic and international policies of the United States on a day-to-day basis and with the personal authority of the president of the United States. He or she would report to the president through the national security adviser. From good organization comes good policy.

In practice, responsibilities for this coordination have recently shifted back from the Treasury Department to the White House. However, there has been no formal designation of the National Security Council's lead role. That should happen forthwith, so leadership on this important issue becomes a matter of institutional permanence rather than a function of individual personalities and relationships. Moreover, such a designation will go a long way toward putting issues regarding terrorist financing front and center in every bilateral diplomatic discussion with every "frontline" state in the fight against terrorism—at every level of the bilateral relationship, including, on a consistent basis, the highest.

No one knows how much money is being spent to combat terrorist financing or whether these expenditures are efficient and effective. Accordingly, the National Security Council and the White House Office of Management and Budget (OMB) should conduct a crosscutting analysis of the budgets of all U.S. government agencies as they relate to terrorist financing. Because we do not today have a clear sense of how many financial and human resources are actually devoted to the various tasks involved in combating terrorist financing, it is impossible to make fully informed, strategic decisions about whether functions are duplicative or resource allocations are optimal. A crosscutting review will enable the president to gain clarity about who is doing what, how well, and with what resources.

In conducting that analysis, provisions should be made to incorporate classified material, so that the full range of activity underway is considered: (1) intelligence collection, analysis, and operations; (2) law enforcement operations (including related operations against money laundering, drug trafficking, and organized crime); (3) regulatory activity, including policy development, enforcement, and international standard setting and implementation; (4) sanctions, including an analysis of their effectiveness as an interdiction and deterrence mechanism; (5) diplomatic activity in support of all of the above; and (6) contributions made by the Defense Department.

U.S. policymakers should seek to build a new framework for U.S.-Saudi relations. The 9/11 Commission, mirroring the Council on Foreign Relations task force, concluded: "The problems in the U.S.-Saudi relationship must be confronted, openly. The United States and Saudi Arabia must determine if they can build a relationship that political leaders on both sides are prepared to publicly defend—a relationship about more than oil. . . . It should include a shared interest in greater tolerance and cultural respect, translating into a commitment to fight the violent extremists who foment hatred."

Congress should enact, and the new president should support, an interagency, Treasury-led certification regime on terrorist financing. Many countries have taken steps to improve their anti–money laundering and counterterrorist fighting regimes, but many have not. Certification regimes have the ability to quickly galvanize action consistent with U.S. interests. Moreover, they require official findings of fact that have the effect of compelling sustained U.S. attention to important concerns. For these reasons, Congress should pass and the president should sign legislation requiring the executive branch to submit to Congress on an annual basis a written certification (classified, if necessary) detailing the steps that foreign nations have taken to cooperate in U.S. and international efforts to combat terrorist financing.

Major changes are needed in the law enforcement, intelligence, military, and financial functions of the U.S. government to strengthen our hand in fighting the jihadists. In addition to speedily implementing the recommendations of the 9/11 Commission, the United States should modify personnel policies in intelligence and law enforcement agencies (notably the CIA and FBI) to facilitate noncareer tracks. The domestic intelligence activities of the FBI should be performed by a distinctly separate new organization within the Bureau. And an independent, outside oversight board, as recommended by the 9/11 Commission, should be established rather than the internal advisory group recently created by executive order.

The U.S. military's special operations forces for counterterrorism activities should be greatly expanded and should be supported by a military organization that maintains a covert—not official cover—presence in other nations to support U.S. military action against terrorists. The military must enhance its capabilities and modify its policies to facilitate small-unit special forces operations, including covert operations, against terrorists. Congress must make clear that it will accept casualties in such operations.

In addition, a special assistant to the president for combating terrorist financing should be designated at the National Security Council with the specific mandate to lead U.S. efforts on terrorist financing issues. Congress should pass and the president should sign legislation requiring the executive branch to submit to Congress on an annual basis a written certification detailing the steps that foreign nations have taken to cooperate in U.S. and international efforts to combat terrorist financing.

7. Homeland Security

Three years after the 9/11 attacks, critical infrastructure in the United States remains as vulnerable as it was three years ago. Chief among those vulnerable systems are ports and shipping containers, rails (both freight and passenger), and chemical plants. In the major metropolitan areas, emergency services personnel (police, fire, medical) continue to lack minimum essential equipment, training, staff, plans, and technologies. Moreover, the current block-grant federal assistance program does not identify minimum essential capabilities or guarantee that basic requirements will ever be met. Finally, there has been no effort to identify the gaps between state and local capabilities and the systems required to address major catastrophic events, such as nuclear or biological attacks.

The 9/11 terrorist attacks highlighted the fact that our borders and oceans are not effective barriers for terrorists who plot to attack within U.S. borders. While American soldiers continue to sacrifice in conflicts overseas, few sacrifices have been undertaken to reduce vulnerabilities at home. This section highlights some of our greatest weaknesses and offers a pragmatic policy response for each.

Securing Ports and Containers

The United States has numerous vulnerabilities, but our 361 seaports, which connect us to the world and handle 90 percent of everything moving in and out of our country, remain especially inviting to terrorists. And, unfortunately, our ports are as critical to homeland security as they are vulnerable to attack. Unsecured ports, and the 16,000 shipping containers that move through them every day, provide terrorists with a means of transporting weapons, people, and potentially deadlier contraband into the United States. In addition, vulnerable ports provide terrorists with a means of bringing the entire international trade system to its knees. In 2002, approximately 7 million containers arrived at U.S. seaports, accounting for more than 75 percent of the U.S. non-North America trade by value and 95 percent by weight. A 2002 simulation of a terrorist attack involving cargo containers demonstrated that if every seaport were shut down temporarily due to such an attack, the estimated loss in revenue to the U.S. economy would be $58 billion.

Because the threat has obvious national security implications, it deserves high-level attention at all levels of government. But the issue continues to receive an insufficient response, despite the importance of global transportation to our national interests and the monumental task of securing and monitoring the 7 million containers shipped through U.S. ports each year. Today, only 2 percent of those containers are inspected.

The key to efficient port security is identifying high-risk containers rapidly and dealing with them effectively, without impeding the flow of container traffic through the port facility. Failing to identify and deal with a high-risk container could be disastrous, but frequently disrupting container traffic could have its own deleterious effects on the economy. Given the volume of container traffic and the difficulty of conducting thorough inspections, meeting these requirements is a tall order.

PRACTICAL LIMITS

Large container ships can receive and discharge more than 6 million pounds of freight in a single hour. Today, the two largest container ports in the world, Hong Kong and Singapore, together handle more than 1 million forty-foot ocean containers each month. Moreover, on the average day, more than 15 million containers are moving by vessel, truck, or train, or awaiting delivery. As mega-container ships capable of carrying upward of 3,000 forty-foot containers were put into operation in the 1990s, the need to choreograph the movement of the boxes in and out of a marine terminal became more time-sensitive. Today's rapidly moving operations make the system very susceptible to disruptions. If many containers get held up in the off-loading process, the trains and trucks carrying boxes to the port will be trapped outside the terminal gate. If they are carrying perishable freight, it will spoil and become useless. The most serious economic blow, however, would be dealt to the manufacturing and retail sectors. Because 90 percent of the world's general cargo moves inside these boxes, when they slow down or stop, so do assembly lines and retailers such as Wal-Mart and Home Depot.

For this reason, inspecting every container that comes through our ports would be impractical. In the aftermath of 9/11, however, legislation was introduced in Congress that would require every container entering the United States to be unloaded and examined. It takes five agents three hours to completely inspect a fully loaded forty-foot cargo container. On an average day, 18,000 containers are off-loaded in the ports of Los Angeles and Long Beach, California, alone. If every box were unloaded and inspected, meeting the proposed 100-percent inspection mandate would translate into 270,000 man-hours per day—which would require more than three times the customs inspection manpower that currently exists nationwide.

Moreover, even if we could inspect every container that came through our ports, container security would still not be ensured. On average, overseas containers will pass through seventeen intermediate points before they arrive at their final U.S. destination, and often their contents come from several locations before they are even loaded into the box. Nearly 40 percent of all containers shipped to the United States are the maritime transportation equivalent of the back of a United Parcel Service (UPS) van. Intermediaries, known as consolidators, gather goods or packages from a variety of customers or even other intermediaries and load them all into the container. Just like express carriers in the United States, they only know what their customers tell them about what they are shipping. Explosives, even weapons of mass destruction, could easily be loaded into a container at its point of origin or anywhere along the way to the marine terminal. Port terminal operators have no way of confirming whether what is advertised as the contents of a box is what is actually in it.

SECURING CONTAINERS IN THREE STEPS

Securing cargo containers requires three steps. First, only authorized goods should be allowed to be loaded into a container. Second, once a container is moving within the global transportation system, the shipment should be impervious to an unauthorized breach. Third, each port should be capable of rapidly inspecting any cargo containers that arouse suspicion.

The U.S. government has taken numerous steps since the 9/11 attacks to improve container and port security. The International Ship and Port Facility Security Code (ISPS) recently came into force, marking the dawn of a new age for maritime security. Now, 22,539 vessels and the 7,974 port facilities that serve as their on-ramps and off-ramps should be abiding by new security measures adopted by the International Maritime Organization. Congress gave the code the force of law when it adopted the Maritime Transportation Security Act of 2002. But the new mandate has not come with the resources required to meet it. Since 9/11, Washington has provided only $516 million toward the $5.6 billion the Coast Guard estimates U.S. ports need to make them minimally secure. In the fiscal 2005 budget, the White House asked for just $50 million more. Given the severe constraints on the state and local budgets within the jurisdictions where America's commercial seaports are located, it is difficult to see how these ports will be able to afford the new security requirements.

Another program, the Container Security Initiative (CSI) places Customs and Border Protection (CBP) staff at the largest foreign seaports to identify and inspect high-risk containers before they are shipped to the United States. Over twenty-four ports, including all the largest seaports in the world, have signed agreements to participate in the CSI program. However, CBP is staffing the CSI program by sending teams of just four to eight inspectors on temporary duty assignments of three to four months because the White House has not authorized the overseas billets for longer assignments. Inspectors are receiving no formal language or other training to prepare them for these overseas postings. Given that the teams are so small—only eight inspectors in Hong Kong, which is the world largest port—they are able to inspect only the tiniest of percentages of containers. Moreover, CSI uses ships' manifest data, which the Government Accountability Office (GAO) called "one of the least reliable or useful for targeting purposes," to evaluate risk.

The CBP also uses the National Targeting Center to alert customs inspectors in a port to hold selected boxes until they can be examined. Using the Automated Targeting System (ATS), the National Targeting Center evaluates information found on the cargo container manifest and the customs declaration form and correlates it with intelligence. CBP officials then use this information to identify high-risk containers for additional scrutiny. Although the ATS was originally designed to identify illegal narcotics shipments, it has been modified to identify many more types of illegal contraband.

CBP also employs the Supply Chain Stratified Examination, which randomly selects containers for inspection. CBP officials have the capacity to conduct a nonintrusive inspection with equipment such as the Vehicle and Cargo Inspection System (VACIS), which takes a gamma-ray image of the target container. This system cuts down on inspection man-hours by distinguishing between trusted and untrusted boxes.

The Customs-Trade Partnership Against Terrorism (C-TPAT) is a cooperative program between CBP and members of the international trade community in which private companies agree to improve the security of their supply chains in return for a reduced likelihood that their containers will be inspected. By the end of 2003, 4,600 importers, ocean carriers, and freight forwarders had submitted applications to join C-TPAT.

The speed with which the CSI and C-TPAT initiatives have been embraced is not difficult to explain. Both importers and foreign port authorities fear that U.S. inspectors will subject shipments from non-participating companies and ports to greater scrutiny, with the associated delays. But these fears are largely unfounded, because the Bureau of Customs and Border Protection lacks the manpower and resources to adequately staff the CSI, to review applications of companies that wish to participate in C-TPAT, and to move away from error-prone cargo manifests that remain the cornerstone of the targeting system.

A NEW PLAN

The shipping networks we rely on today are integrated into much larger global systems. Thus, to fully secure our ports and the integrity of our global transportation system, we would need to harden all the key nodes in the transportation network. America's borders represent only a territorial line where our sovereign jurisdiction begins, but the threat to container security starts much farther back.

Virtually all containers coming into the United States pass through a few foreign seaports. In fact, approximately 70 percent of the 8 million containers that arrived in U.S. ports in 2002 originated from or moved through four overseas terminal operators. These operators, Hutchinson

Port Holdings, P&O Ports, PSA Corporation, and Maersk-Sealand, are the second-to-last line of defense, and they should ensure that only secure boxes are loaded on ships that cross the Atlantic and Pacific oceans. Their job would involve two steps. First, they should confirm that a low-risk container is in fact low-risk; if it is deemed high-risk, it should be handled in a way that minimizes danger and disruption.

Guaranteeing that a container has not been tampered with will become much easier if we can ensure that the container was loaded in a secure facility at its point of origin. Secure facilities should have loading docks with safeguards that prevent anyone from gaining unauthorized entry. When the container is being loaded, digital photographs with time signatures could record the interior of the container at four stages: when it is empty, half full, full, and after the security seal is activated. These photographs would be stored on a data chip with the container or be transmitted electronically to the authorities in the loading port. The container could have additional sensors: light, temperature, and pressure sensors that could detect an unauthorized intrusion, and internal sensors that could detect gamma or neutron emissions associated with a nuclear or dirty bomb, prohibited chemical and biological agents, or the carbon dioxide generated by smuggled persons.

Using global positioning system (GPS) technology, the container's route could be tracked over sea and land. When in transit over land, if a truck driver is going through areas known for smuggling or terrorist activities, a form of invisible fence technology could be outfitted inside the truck. A microcomputer could detect whether the truck strayed from its route, send an alert message to the relevant authorities, and later automatically idle the engine before the truck arrived at the port terminal.

When a container arrives at a terminal, an inspection unit would create a CAT scan-style image of its contents, detect any radiation, and gather information from the container's sensors, and do all of this nonintrusively. These data would be forwarded electronically to all the national customs authorities along the route. With multiple sets of eyes monitoring containers en route, the chance of a high-risk container penetrating the system would be dramatically reduced.

To ensure that each container is traveling on its advertised route, authorities will need to track the shipment over sea and land. Most Americans would be surprised to learn that although civilian air-traffic controllers can track aircraft, there is no equivalent system for monitoring movement of ocean-going ships, let alone the containers aboard those ships. Creating this capability is technologically feasible, but it has never been mandated. Although large ships must carry a device that allows the Coast Guard to detect them when they are near U.S. shores, the device can only track ships within twenty to thirty miles of the coast.

There are several ways the U.S. government could establish a container tracking system. The first option is to use a GPS-based system that would send a signal to a transmitter on each container and receive a signal from that transmitter regarding its location, using a different technology. The second option is to place Radio Frequency Identification (RFID) tags on each container, which would be able to receive and send transmissions, but only when the container is moving through "choke points" at marine and terrestrial terminals. The third option is to use space-based radars to establish "globally persistent" surveillance systems that can provide a real-time picture of anything that can be seen from space. This technology is not currently available for the container security task. But were it to be developed for such a task, it would provide the greatest resolution and tracking capability of all three options.

Using new technologies and procedures to check and double-check containers will serve several purposes. First, they will create a deterrent against terrorists shipping a nuclear weapon in a container. With increased scrutiny of containers via sensors and more vigorous monitoring, we could push the probability of detection from its current 10-percent range into the 90-percent range. Given the difficulty of obtaining a nuclear weapon, a terrorist organization would be less likely to take such a risk. Outfitting containers so they could be tracked would provide the means to act on intelligence about high-risk containers without disrupting the rest of the transportation system.

The cost for all this would be reasonable. Assuming that the average container is used for ten years, the initial cost of installing sensor technology into the box would add about $5 to the price of each shipment. The latest radiation-detection portals and container-scanning equipment units cost about $1 million each. Large ports would need several to ensure that the screening process would not slow the flow of container traffic. Ports should also have spares on hand to allow for routine maintenance. New command centers with upgraded technology and good analysts would be the backbone of a secure network to share and analyze the scanned images across multiple jurisdictions.

Some of the costs of security can be passed on to the private sector by providing appropriate incentives. One initiative could be establishing "green lanes" in seaports. The green lane would be similar to the E-Z Pass toll collection system on the highway. A green lane in a seaport would be authorized only for secure containers whose location could be tracked. The benefits to the shipper would come in several ways. First, the users of the green lane would be provided with assurances from the U.S. authorities that these boxes would receive preferential treatment if their shipment were targeted for inspection, thereby minimizing delays for that shipper. Second, should the United States temporarily have to shut down ports following a terrorist attack, once the ports were reopened those shippers with green lane privileges would be authorized to move first.

SECURING OUR TRAINS

The Madrid commuter train attacks that killed 191 people on March 11, 2004, exposed the extreme vulnerability of public transportation systems. Since the attacks, the U.S. Transportation Security Administration (TSA) has been testing more rigorous security measures on some commuter trains, including bomb-screening machines, random bag checks, and patrols with bomb-sniffing dogs. These efforts are sporadic, however, and the U.S. government has not allocated funding necessary for sustained and effective security measures.

Journalists from ABC News ran an experiment in September 2004 to assess security on commuter trains in the United States. The journalists were able to leave several backpacks conspicuously unattended, à la Madrid, in three different commuter trains in Washington, D.C., Virginia, and New York, without raising suspicion, for two hours in one case. Although security is slowly improving, terrorists could very easily attack many vulnerable points in our system.

The 32 million Americans who use public transportation every day deserve more thorough protection from terrorist attacks. An American Public Transportation Association (APTA) survey found that the United States will have to spend $6 billion to secure the nation's transit systems. Since 9/11, however, only $155 million has been appropriated by

Congress for this effort—which is about 1 percent of the funding appropriated for aviation security, even though every day sixteen times as many people travel by public transportation as by air.

Although Congress has introduced legislation designed to increase transportation security, including block-grant programs, a number of congressional leaders have delayed passage of the bills. The next administration has the opportunity to play a critical role in this process by ensuring the passage of a block-grant program dedicated to enhancing transit system security, focusing in particular on subways, commuter trains, and Amtrak railways.

SECURING CHEMICAL FACILITIES

According to the Environmental Protection Agency, there are 7,728 U.S. chemical plants in which an accident—or act of sabotage—could endanger 1,000 or more nearby residents. Of those, 123 facilities could threaten more than 1 million people. More recent assessments by the Department of Homeland Security (DHS) conclude that the number of plants threatening 1,000 or more people has been lowered to 4,391, while the number potentially affecting more than 1 million has dropped to two. A GAO report released in March 2003 noted that even though U.S. chemical facilities were "attractive targets for terrorists," the ability of any facility to respond to an attack was "unknown." The GAO found that the chemical industry was not required by law to assess vulnerabilities or take action to secure its facilities and that "the federal government has not comprehensively assessed the chemical industry's vulnerabilities to terrorist attacks." The problem is that the efforts are ultimately dependent on the willingness of plant owners and managers to work with Homeland Security officials and spend money and time on the efforts. DHS currently has no ability to force security measures on the industry.

The Justice Department calls the threat "real and credible." Yet the chemical industry is not required by law to assess vulnerabilities or secure its facilities. The *Richmond Times-Dispatch* reported that "the Environmental Protection Agency recently tried to impose stricter security standards on chemical manufacturers, but it backed down after the industry balked."[1]

SUPPORTING EMERGENCY RESPONDERS

Local and state emergency responders are a vital component of America's front line in homeland security. First responders play a central role in managing the immediate response to a terrorist attack, and their efforts in the initial minutes following an attack will determine how many lives are saved and how quickly order is restored. The nation's emergency responders, like military field medics, have been asked to place themselves in harm's way to defend and rescue the wounded on the battlefield of the twenty-first century. Unfortunately, America's emergency responders are underfunded and, as a result, unprepared for this duty. If the next administration does not take immediate steps to improve emergency responder capabilities, then the next attack on the U.S. homeland could be even more disastrous than the attacks on 9/11.

An independent task force, sponsored by the Council on Foreign Relations, issued a publication, "Emergency Responders: Drastically Underfunded, Dangerously Unprepared," which offers (1) a glimpse of America's critical deficits in emergency preparedness, and (2) recommendations for making up these deficits.

Before highlighting the deficiencies in our emergency responder system, it is important to note that since 9/11, the United States has made significant improvements in emergency preparedness. In March 2002, the Department of Homeland Security was established, and this effort was coupled with increased funding for emergency preparedness at the federal, state, and local levels and increased training for emergency response personnel. These initiatives are important and useful, but they are a far cry from what America requires to respond to the catastrophic emergencies, such as those involving chemical, biological, radiological, or nuclear agents, that now loom on the horizon.

To improve our emergency preparedness, we first need to strengthen the foundations of our emergency response system. Before we establish a higher bar for the emergency response system, we should first meet the current bar. For example, two-thirds of fire departments nationwide do not meet the consensus fire-service standard for minimum safe staffing levels. On average, fire departments have only 50 percent of the radios and one-third of the breathing apparatuses they need to equip all of the firefighters on one shift. Public health systems nationwide are underfunded and cannot meet the standards that they are increasingly required to meet.

An urgent task is to define, and then assess, the country's minimum essential capabilities for emergency responders. There is currently no systematic national standard of essential capabilities and therefore no way to assess how much progress we are making toward preparedness on the federal, state, or local level. More important, there is currently no way of determining which jurisdictions are suffering from critical gaps in preparedness and what steps those jurisdictions should be taking to make up the gaps. Once we have assessed our emergency preparedness, we can set systematic requirements for emergency responder systems nationwide, codified in national capability standards. The capability standards should include guidelines for burden sharing among federal, state, and local jurisdictions. Although the federal government should not be responsible for normal spending on emergency readiness and public health at the state and local levels, federal funds should be used to help state and local governments meet the essential standards for preparedness, uniquely designed to prepare jurisdictions for catastrophic terrorist attacks.

Improving emergency preparedness also requires that we provide the funds necessary to equip and train emergency responders and implement programs critical to responding to mass destruction events. According to the Council on Foreign Relations' task force, the United States will fall approximately $98.4 billion short of meeting emergency responder needs over the next five years if current funding levels are maintained. These shortfalls in funding translate into dangerous deficits, given the scope and character of the terrorism threat. For example, only 10 percent of fire departments nationwide have personnel and equipment to handle a building collapse; police departments throughout the United States do not have protective gear required to secure a site after an attack with weapons of mass destruction (WMD); public health laboratories in most states do not have the basic equipment to adequately respond to chemical or biological attacks; and most cities do not have the equipment needed to determine which hazardous agents emergency responders are facing following an attack.

Other programs the task force factors into "emergency responder needs" include implementing a nationwide emergency–911 system with wireless capability; enhancing urban search and rescue capabilities of major cities in cases where buildings or other large structures collapse; implementing interoperable communications systems for emergency responders; enhancing public health preparedness by strengthening laboratories, disease tracking, and training for public health personnel for dealing with biological, chemical, and radiological events; providing protective gear and WMD remediation equipment to firefighters; enhancing emergency agricultural and veterinary capabilities to respond to a national food supply attack; and enhancing the surge capacity of the nation's hospitals.

Specialized training for emergency personnel and sustaining equipment capabilities over time are also required to be fully prepared. New equipment will only have a marginal effect on preparedness if personnel are not trained to use it effectively or if it is not maintained well. In fact, many state and local governments have been unwilling to accept federal funding for programs that will generate long-term costs without the promise of federal funding to cover those costs. Because state and local governments will continue to leave themselves unprepared for fear of getting stuck with the bill, the U.S. government needs to guarantee sustained multiyear funding for critical preparedness programs.

Federal funding of state and local homeland security should be requirements-based. For each major metropolitan area, there should be a clear target of minimum essential capabilities to respond to a catastrophic terrorist attack and a multiyear funding plan to achieve those minimum essential capabilities.

Refocusing our funding priorities is another way to keep our emergency preparedness programs cost effective. For example, the U.S. government currently disburses emergency preparedness funds according to a minimum level due to each state, plus additional funds based on a state's population. This formula has led to some very uneven funding. Wyoming receives $10 per capita while New York state receives $1.40 per capita, from the Department of Homeland Security. Although all Americans are equally deserving of protection, some Americans live in high-risk areas and some in lower-risk areas, and preparedness funding should reflect this reality.

Improving emergency preparedness also requires that the U.S. government swiftly deliver assistance and funding to state and local governments. According to the Council on Foreign Relations task force, many metropolitan areas and states have actually received and spent a small portion of their congressionally appropriated emergency responder funds. State and local governments have complained that the increased amounts of paperwork, coupled with shifting federal requirements, have made accessing and efficiently spending preparedness funds difficult. According to the National Emergency Managers Association, "appropriation cycles have been erratic, causing extreme burdens on state and local governments to continue preparedness activities when there is no federal funding, and then forcing them to thoughtfully and strategically apply several years of federal funds and millions of dollars at one time."[2]

The U.S. government should also apply itself to disseminating best practices throughout the emergency responder communities. There is currently no formal mechanism through which emergency responders can share best practices and lessons learned, though the emergency responder community has expressed a great deal of interest in the idea. Centralizing and cataloging these data would surely improve the near-term quality of our response efforts and provide a long-term foundation upon which to base decisions about priorities, planning, training, and equipment.

If terrorists employ biological, chemical, or radiological agents in a catastrophic attack, the emergency response and rescue operations would be orders of magnitude more difficult and dangerous than those following 9/11. Improving our emergency preparedness by swiftly addressing funding and planning shortfalls may dramatically decrease civilian and emergency responder casualties should such an event transpire. September 11 demonstrated the great sacrifice our emergency responders have made, and continue to make, for America. To ensure that their continued sacrifice is not made in vain, we should provide them with the equipment and training they require to effectively and safely fulfill their duty.

8. Preventing Nuclear Terror

The problem of terrorists utilizing nuclear weapons is the classic case of a low probability/high consequence policy conundrum. Terrorists almost certainly cannot build a nuclear weapon, and it had been unlikely that they would obtain one from a nation state. Unfortunately, the proliferation of nuclear weapons to Pakistan, North Korea, and Iran now increases the likelihood of terrorists obtaining a nuclear device. Controls on the Russian nuclear inventory also are a source of concern. If terrorists did obtain and utilize a nuclear weapon, the results could be extremely catastrophic and hard to overestimate. The problem may be simply stated:

- Nonproliferation and counterproliferation have not successfully eliminated the threat of terrorist access to nuclear weapons or materials.

- Deterring terrorists with the objective of causing mass casualties will be extremely difficult, if not impossible.

- Upgrading domestic preparedness for nuclear terrorism will (1) be expensive, and (2) only slightly improve the chances of preventing an attack.

From a policy perspective, preventing nuclear terrorism is unique. Political historians would be challenged to find a policy problem in which all political perspectives agree that the scope of the problem is enormous, the policy solutions widely recognized and accepted, and yet the progress of implementing solutions so painfully and dangerously slow.

This chapter (1) analyzes the potential sources of nuclear material and weapons that could be acquired by terrorist organizations and what we are doing to prevent that from happening, (2) assesses current domestic efforts to prevent a nuclear terrorist attack, and (3) proposes specific policy options that address multiple aspects of the threat.

THE THREAT IS REAL

We can safely assume that terrorist organizations as well funded as al Qaeda wish to gain access to either a nuclear weapon or to fissile material. Despite the destruction of their headquarters and training ground in Afghanistan, al Qaeda's network is still capable of "catastrophic attacks." CIA director George Tenet confirmed that al Qaeda has repeatedly sought to acquire a nuclear device. Earlier this year, he told the Senate Intelligence Committee that attacking the United States with nuclear weapons remains a "religious obligation" in Osama bin Laden's eyes.[1]

Despite almost universal acceptance among intelligence analysts that terrorists have tried to acquire and would readily use nuclear weapons, supporting open-source evidence is scant. However, one well-documented episode involving al Qaeda and Pakistani nuclear experts illustrates the point. According to the *Washington Post,* in August 2001, bin Laden met with two key former officials from Pakistan's nuclear weapons program. Over the course of three days of intense discussion, he and Ayman al-Zawahri quizzed Sultan Bashiruddin Mahmood and Abdul Majeed about chemical, biological, and especially nuclear weapons.[2] Al Qaeda had sought out Mahmood, one of Pakistan's leading specialists in uranium enrichment, for his capabilities, his convictions, and his connections. Mahmood's career spanned thirty years at the Pakistani Atomic Energy Commission, and he had been a key figure at the Kahuta plant that had produced the enriched uranium for Pakistan's first nuclear bomb in 1998. After his forced departure from Pakistan's Atomic Energy Agency in 1999, Mahmood founded a "charitable agency" with Majeed, who had served as director of Pakistan's Atomic Energy Commission. Ominously, Mahmood predicted in an essay that "by 2002, millions may die through mass destruction weapons, terrorist attacks, and suicide."[3]

Mahmood and Majeed were arrested in October of 2003 and questioned by joint Pakistani-CIA teams. According to Mahmood, bin Laden was particularly interested in nuclear weapons. Bin Laden's colleagues told the Pakistani scientists that al Qaeda had succeeded in acquiring nuclear material for a bomb from the Islamic Movement of Uzbekistan. Mahmood explained to his hosts that the material in question could be used only in a "dirty bomb." Al-Zawahri and the others then sought Mahmood's help in recruiting other Pakistani nuclear experts who could provide uranium of the required purity, as well as assistance in constructing a nuclear weapon. Pakistani officials indicated that Mahmood and Majeed "spoke extensively about weapons of mass destruction" and provided detailed responses to bin Laden's questions about the manufacture of nuclear, biological, and chemical weapons.[4]

In the end, U.S. intelligence agencies have concluded that Mahmood and Majeed had provided bin Laden with a blueprint for constructing nuclear weapons. The CIA's summary of the matter, according to President Bush, concluded that although Mahmood and his charity claimed "to serve the hungry and needy of Afghanistan," in fact they "provided information about nuclear weapons to Al Qaeda."[5]

LOOKING FOR NUKES?

There are three main sources through which al Qaeda or similar organizations could acquire nuclear weapons:

THEFT: The single largest potential source of nuclear devices and fissionable material is the storage houses of the former Soviet Union. Fissile material from the former Soviet Union has been intercepted on seven different occasions in Europe since the end of the Cold War.[6] The remaining material is poorly guarded, and both theft and corruption pose threats to U.S. interests.

BLACK-MARKET PURCHASE: The Pakistani "Father of the Islamic Bomb," A. Q. Kahn, openly admitted that he had developed a nuclear proliferation–based business. The magnitude and ease with which he perpetrated the proliferation of weapons blueprints, parts used to enrich uranium for weapons, and nuclear expertise to countries such as North Korea, Iran, and Libya demonstrates the danger of the black market.

STATE SPONSORSHIP: As early as 1987, the International Task Force on Prevention of Nuclear Terrorism reached the conclusion that state sponsorship was increasing the probability of nuclear terrorism. States such as North Korea and Iran have aggressively sought to acquire nuclear weapons and have simultaneously sponsored terrorism.[7]

RUSSIA: Nuclear weapons and material from Russia offer terrorists the best opportunity to secure the necessary resources for an attack. At the end of the Cold War, 22,000 tactical nuclear weapons remained in fourteen of the fifteen newly independent states of the former Soviet Union. The small, relatively easily portable weapons played an integral role in the defensive strategy of the Soviet military units stationed there.[8] In 1991, Dick Cheney, the U.S. secretary of defense at the time, observed that recovery of 99 percent of the weapons would constitute "excellent" performance.[9] But the loss of even 1 percent would have left 220 weapons unaccounted for and available to terrorist organizations.

In its February 2002 report to Congress on nuclear risks from Russia, the National Intelligence Council—the organization responsible for the U.S. intelligence community's most authoritative judgments—confirmed four cases between 1992 and 1999 in which "weapons-grade and weapons-usable nuclear materials have been stolen from some Russian institutes." The bottom line: "Undetected smuggling has occurred, although we do not know the extent or magnitude."[10]

Skeptics say that the threat of terrorists securing a nuclear capability in Russia is overstated, and our Nunn-Lugar proliferation prevention money there ill-spent. The recent spate of terrorist attacks in Russia, including the horrific attack on the school in Beslan, suggests otherwise. During the height of the terror crisis in September, 2004, President Vladimir Putin ordered the deployment of extra troops to guard dozens of nuclear facilities across the country. "After the latest terrorist attacks, security services decided to send more interior ministry troops to all nuclear sites across the country," a Russian Atomic Energy Agency spokesman said.[11] Clearly, a nation confident about the security of its nukes would not rush to reinforce facilities during a major crisis.

PAKISTAN: Recent revelations that Pakistan's "Father of the Islamic Bomb," Dr. A. Q. Kahn, assisted Iran, North Korea, and Libya in developing their nuclear weapons programs has greatly shaken the faith in Pakistani leader Pervez Musharraf. Rather than prosecuting Kahn and the extensive network of personnel who supported his proliferation activities, Musharraf granted Kahn a pardon. Although Musharraf claimed that Kahn's popularity as a national hero prevented him from taking stronger measures, evidence strongly supports the assertion that the Pakistani military, and perhaps Musharraf himself, allowed the proliferation.

Kahn openly admitted that two former army chiefs supported his proliferation activities. The magnitude and ease with which the Pakistanis perpetrated the proliferation of weapons blueprints, parts used to enrich uranium for weapons, and nuclear expertise also indicate support from the highest levels of leadership. Musharraf's "reassuring" claim that all proliferation activities ended in the 1990s, before he established the National Command Authority over the nuclear program, should not relieve U.S. concern about this issue.

Pakistan has enough enriched uranium stockpiled for fifty-two more nuclear weapons, in addition to the forty-eight it already deploys. Pakistan is a committed nonsignatory to the Nuclear Non-Proliferation Treaty (NPT) and has declared that it is unprepared to allow any degree of inspection by the International Atomic Energy Association (IAEA).

NORTH KOREA: In October 2002, the North Koreans admitted to the Bush administration that they had developed a secret uranium enrichment program, which was almost certainly based on Pakistan's centrifuge blueprint. By the end of the year, they expelled IAEA inspectors from the country, withdrew from the Nuclear Non-Proliferation Treaty, and began reprocessing the 8,000 spent fuel rods from the Yongbyon nuclear reactor that they had agreed to freeze in 1994—enough for about five or six bombs. As Washington and Pyongyang remain at a stalemate, the North Koreans have been reprocessing plutonium, enriching uranium, and completing construction of facilities that will be able to produce about a dozen nuclear warheads a year.[12]

Given North Korea's well-known reputation for sponsoring organized crime and selling missile technology to anyone with hard currency, and Kim Jung-Il's hatred for the United States, the possibility that the country would provide terrorists with a nuclear capability is not unrealistic.

IRAN: During 2004, Iran has refused to abandon plans to process enriched uranium, an essential step in the development of nuclear weapons, despite pressure from the international community. Although Iran almost certainly does not possess a nuclear capability, the country's sponsorship of terrorist organizations in the past makes it a distinct potential threat in the immediate future.

WORKING TO PREVENT THE WORST
WHERE ARE WE NOW?

The National Security Strategy, released by the Bush administration in September 2002, identifies terrorists armed with weapons of mass destruction as the "gravest danger" facing the United States. In order to address that threat, the administration formulated the much-debated doctrine of preemptive strike. In sum, the United States must be prepared to stop "rogue states and their terrorist clients" before they threaten to use WMD.[13] Although the flawed intelligence that provided the justification for attacking Iraq has placed the doctrine under increased scrutiny, preemption will likely remain an important part of American counterterrorism policy in the future.

The Nunn-Lugar program was funded in order to prevent the proliferation of weapons and technologies of mass destruction (nuclear, biological, chemical) that had been developed and stockpiled by the Soviet Union. The program has multiple dimensions, ranging from improving security at former Soviet nuclear research facilities and safeguarding used nuclear material to finding productive civilian research and other projects for the scientists and engineers who worked on these programs so they are not tempted to sell their wares (and especially, their brains) to the highest bidder. The program initially started in the Defense Department, but most of the budget now rests with the State Department under the rubric "Cooperative Threat Reduction" (CTR).

The Nunn-Lugar program has proven to be the most effective we have for securing and eliminating nuclear, chemical, and biological weapons in the former Soviet Union. The 9/11 Commission Report weighed in with another important endorsement of the Nunn-Lugar program, saying that "[p]reventing the proliferation of [weapons of mass destruction] warrants a maximum effort—by strengthening counter-proliferation efforts, expanding the Proliferation Security Initiative, and supporting the Cooperative Threat Reduction Program."[14] President Bush, however, cut the funding for the current Nunn-Lugar program in the budget he recently submitted to Congress from $451 million to $409 million.[15]

In many ways, bureaucratic politics make us our own worst enemy when it comes to implementing the foreign policy intended to protect the nation from nuclear terrorism.

Although the State Department leads the interagency policy process on nonproliferation and manages global U.S. nuclear security policy, it does not control the funding or operational aspects of many programs. As with other problems that require extensive interagency cooperation, the lack of strong leadership from the White House, in both the Clinton and Bush administrations, has slowed progress. In the words of Graham Allison, "Today, if the president asked at a Cabinet meeting who is responsible for preventing nuclear terrorism, six or eight hands in the room might go up, or none at all."

Department of Defense efforts under the CTR program focus on providing assistance to the newly independent states of the former Soviet Union in meeting their strategic arms reduction obligations under START I and eliminating or safeguarding their WMD infrastructure. The CTR program has carried out projects in Russia, Ukraine, Belarus, Kazakhstan, Latvia, Lithuania, and Uzbekistan. The Defense Threat Reduction Agency is responsible for threat reduction to the United States and its allies from WMD through the execution of technology security activities.

Programs managed by the Department of Energy (DOE) focus on ensuring the security of Russian nuclear materials, disposing of excess fissile materials, and preventing the "brain drain" of Russian nuclear scientists. Key activities include the Materials Protection, Control, and Accounting (MPC&A) program, which improves the security of fissile materials in the newly independent states by providing security upgrades to selected nuclear facilities, promoting consolidation of nuclear materials in central sites, and improving nuclear materials accounting procedures. The DOE also runs two initiatives that seek to provide alternative employment opportunities for past workers of the Russian nuclear industrial complex, reducing the risk that individual scientists might transfer weapon design know-how to countries of concern.

The Proliferation Security Initiative (PSI), led by the State Department, was developed by the Bush administration in response to the growing challenge posed by the proliferation of weapons of mass destruction, their delivery systems, and related materials worldwide. The PSI seeks to involve in some capacity all states that have a stake in nonproliferation and the ability and willingness to take steps to stop the flow of such items at sea, in the air, or on land. The PSI also seeks cooperation from any state whose vessels, flags, ports, territorial waters, airspace, or land might be used for proliferation purposes by states and nonstate actors.

In March 2001, six months before 9/11, national intelligence officer Robert Walpole testified to a Senate subcommittee, "Non-missile delivery means [of a weapon of mass destruction] are less costly, easier to acquire, and more reliable and accurate."[16] The United States would clearly prefer to prevent terrorists from acquiring the means to attack before they reach the homeland; however, we must be prepared for the strong possibility that our foreign policy efforts will not succeed entirely.

Compared with the overall budget for defense spending, the amount dedicated to guarding against the threat of nuclear terrorism at home is small. In 2004, spending on WMD has amounted to approximately $4 billion of the $40 billion in the DHS budget, whereas the counterproliferation programs of the Defense Department amount to $2 billion of its $400 billion budget.

Acquiring a nuclear weapon is still difficult, but there is a high probability that terrorist organizations such as al Qaeda already possess the capability to develop radiological weapons, or "dirty bombs." In November, 1995, for example, Chechen terrorists threatened to detonate a package containing radioactive Cesium 137 in a Moscow park. Radiological bombs cannot cause mass casualties, but their radiation can cause long-term illness, psychological terror, and limited access to key facilities for an extended period.

The genuine threat of both nuclear and radiological attack makes a viable and effective response absolutely essential. Nuclear Emergency Search Teams (NEST) play a critical role. The mission of NEST is to assess the likelihood of nuclear threats, find nuclear devices, and disable them. A "volunteer fire department for the atomic age," NEST personnel include 1,000 highly trained volunteers, including physicists, engineers, chemists, and mathematicians, who work throughout the country in nuclear laboratories and with private contractors. When deployed to investigate a potential nuclear incident, these "nuclear ninjas" often disguise themselves as tourists or local residents, with their gamma ray and neutron detectors hidden inside briefcases, beer coolers, or book bags.

RECOMMENDATIONS

Although many policy refinements would improve our battle to prevent nuclear terrorism, the starting point for any decisive change must be leadership. In conceiving, organizing, and orchestrating the elements of the U.S. government to focus intensely on the nuclear terrorism issue, one person must have lead responsibility and be held accountable. One commonly discussed notion for improving the U.S. effort on this front is to establish a "czar" to establish policies, priorities, and objectives for combating WMD proliferation, as well as to set budgets and guidelines for cooperation among the various federal agencies and departments involved. In his latest book, *Nuclear Terrorism: The Ultimate Preventable Catastrophe,* Graham Allison stated: "The president should appoint an individual of stature who reports directly to him as his commander in a real war on nuclear terrorism." Although the idea has been much discussed, much more work is needed on how to operationalize such a notion.

Meanwhile, the first line of defense against nuclear terrorism should include nonproliferation regimes, export controls, and diplomatic sanctions. Initiatives to enhance nonproliferation should include:

DENIAL: Efforts should be increased to deny access to nuclear weapons for the "have-nots" of the Nuclear Non-Proliferation Treaty, since horizontal proliferation increases the risk of terrorist access to nuclear weapons. The present international export regime is insufficient and should be tightened. The acceptance of the "peaceful atom" creates ambiguity, and the export of nuclear dual-use material to countries under suspicion could be banned.

DISARMAMENT: The United States should offer to purchase Russia's nuclear material (at a cost of $4 billion per year for five years) to reduce the threat of loose nukes from Russia. Additional efforts could address the weakness of the enforcement and verification mechanisms of the Nuclear Non-Proliferation Treaty and aim at increasing the international tools for actively disarming proliferators.

DIPLOMACY: The United States should pursue international and bilateral sanctions against proliferating states such as North Korea and Iran by terminating international aid and trade while offering relief upon termination of nuclear programs.

A new National Strategy to Combat WMD should emphasize the need for counterproliferation initiatives. Further initiatives to enhance counterproliferation could include:

DEFUSING: The Nunn-Lugar program could be expanded from subsidizing the safeguarding of the fissile material of the former Soviet Union to the collection of enriched uranium worldwide. To effectively meet this objective, resources allocated would have to be considerable and could be in the range of $1 billion to $5 billion annually.

DETERRENCE: The United States should continue to threaten state and nonstate actors that coddle potential nuclear terrorists with massive retaliation upon use of nuclear weapons against the United States.

9. Ensuring Energy Independence

In a period of great volatility and uncertainty in world energy markets, the term "security" is not always easily understood. When speaking about national security in general, George Kennan offered the definition that perhaps best applies to energy security policy today: "the continued ability of this country to pursue its internal life without serious interference."[1]

By Kennan's definition, our reliance on foreign energy imports, and petroleum specifically, clearly threatens our national security. The prospect of a continued disruption, for whatever the reason, raises the prospect of serious interference in the ability of the United States to pursue its internal life and national interests.[2] Although the United States controls just 3 percent of the world's oil reserves, we currently consume 25 percent of the world's oil. As a result of this imbalance, we are heavily reliant on foreign oil, much of which comes from the conflict-ridden Middle East.[3] "As long as we depend on oil, we will depend on Middle East oil," says Fareed Mohamedi, chief economist at PFC Energy.[4] The doubling of Chinese demand for oil over the last ten years has increased the volatility of the energy market. China has now overtaken Japan as the world's second-largest consumer of oil, behind the United States. Chinese decisions on imports and trading links, for both oil and natural gas, will continue to be a major influence on the world energy scene.[5]

Since the 1973 Arab oil embargo, American political leaders have often promised action to reduce U.S. dependence on imported oil. Their efforts have clearly not succeeded. Today, the United States imports more than half of its oil. Since 1973, oil imports have doubled and natural gas imports have increased fourfold. Domestic oil production has declined 15 percent over the past decade; as a result, imports are expected to grow.[6] The bottom line: The greater our dependence on foreign oil, the greater our exposure to the will of other nations and terrorists. World events in 2004, including violence in Iraq, terrorist attacks in Saudi Arabia, and political maneuvering in Russia, all strongly affected the price of oil and, more important, demonstrate the vulnerability of the United States. As oil demand in North America and China continues to climb, we must assess the future stability of the U.S. oil supply.

SAUDI ARABIA

According to the *Petroleum Economist,* "The consequences of a disruption to Saudi oil supplies amid already tight supply and demand conditions would be devastating for the global economy."[7] Saudi Arabia takes the security of its oil very seriously. Although details of the kingdom's security budget are classified, analysts estimate the Saudis spent around $5.5 billion in 2003 and increased security expenditures by 50 percent this year. According to a recent assessment in *Jane's Intelligence Review,* in the past two years the Saudi government has allocated an extra $750 million to enhance security at all its facilities. Although this may seem comforting at first glance, basic economics teaches us that those costs will clearly be transferred to the biggest consumers, particularly the United States.

In the spring of 2004, however, the growing band of jihadists in Saudi Arabia succeeded in sending shock waves through the global energy industry without even firing a single shot at any physical oil infrastructure. A twenty-five-hour rampage of attacks on foreign oil-workers in Al-Khobar, the heart of Saudi refining operations, topped a month of increasingly bloody attacks that seemed to mark an intensification of the militants' campaign against Western interests in the kingdom.

Maritime attacks offer probably the best chance of disrupting the export of oil supplies in a prolonged way. A string of al Qaeda–linked attacks since 1999 suggests a willingness to use sea routes to go after key targets. In 2000, al Qaeda operatives succeeded in launching a suicide attack on the USS *Cole* warship, anchored off Aden, Yemen. In October 2002, al Qaeda militants attacked the French-registered oil tanker *Limburg.*[8]

RUSSIA

In 2002, Russia became the world's largest oil producer, pushing Saudi Arabia into second place, by extracting some 7.28 million barrels per day, compared to the desert kingdom's 7.19 million.[9] In light of that fact, President Bush in 2002 launched discussions with Russian president Vladimir Putin aimed at increasing U.S.-Russian energy trade. Events in Russia since then illustrate that Russia not only exerts significant leverage on world energy security but will continue to build its influence.

During the last two years, President Putin has consolidated state control over critical energy assets. The state's recent acquisition of a majority share in Gazprom gives Putin and his coterie a powerful lever over both domestic and world energy policy. According to the *Economist,* "Putin's energy policy allows Russia to play its neighbors like an orchestra." China and Japan have vied for years to be the destination for an oil pipeline out of Siberia.[10] Gazprom has subsidiaries, wholly or partly owned, throughout the former Soviet Union and in most European countries. The mere threat of cutting off or rerouting oil and gas supplies sends petroleum futures climbing. For example, when Putin announced in September 2004 that Russia would need to temporarily halt exports to China, prices immediately rose. Furthermore, the ability of Chechen terrorists to implement multiple attacks, including the massacre in Beslan, demonstrates that energy supplies from Russia could easily be disrupted.

Because U.S. dependence on Middle East oil complicates our response to security issues in the region, the U.S. government should appropriate significantly more funds to subsidize a rapid shift to energy sources that do not rely upon oil and gas. Market forces have not adequately shifted U.S. reliance upon foreign fossil fuels and are unlikely to do so in a sufficiently timely manner to reduce the risks posed to the U.S. economy and national security.

The completion of the presidential campaign, the inauguration of a new administration, and the convening of a new Congress present an opportunity to rethink fundamentally how we have been fighting against the jihadists. Despite the lack of a major terrorist attack within our borders since 2001, evidence is abundant that the ranks of the jihadists have grown significantly. They have been conducting far more attacks worldwide than before 2001—a clear warning sign that our policies are not working and may even be counterproductive in some cases.

The plan of action laid out in this report is ambitious, complex, and expensive. But the challenge posed by the jihadists fundamentally threatens our nation and the world order, and seems sure to be with us for more than a generation. During World War II and the Cold War, the United States and its allies triumphed over comparably grave threats through fortitude, ingenuity, and substantial sacrifice. We will triumph again over the jihadists. But to do so will require a much greater demonstration of our national strengths than we have put forward to date.

APPENDIX:
RECENT TERRORIST ATTACKS BY REGION

REGION: IRAQ DATE(S)	LOCATION	TARGET	CASUALTIES	GROUP	ATTACK METHOD
August 7, 2003	Baghdad	Jordanian Embassy	19 dead, 65 wounded	Abu Mus'ab al-Zarqawi	Suicide car bomb
August 19, 2003	Baghdad	UN Headquarters	24 dead, including UN envoy Sergio Vieira de Mello, 100 wounded	Abu Mus'ab al-Zarqawi	Suicide truck bomb
August 29, 2003	An Najaf, Shrine of the Imam Ali mosque	Shia cleric Ayatollah Mohammed Bakir al-Hakim	82 dead, 140+ wounded	Abu Mus'ab al-Zarqawi	Suicide car bomb
September 20, 2003	Baghdad	Assassination of IGC member Akila Hashimi	1 dead; Hashimi died of gunshot wounds September 25	Unknown	Gunfire
September 22, 2003	Baghdad	UN Headquarters	1 dead, 19 wounded	Probably Abu Mus'ab al-Zarqawi	Suicide car bomb
October 12, 2003	Baghdad	Baghdad Hotel—houses Westerners	6 dead, 32 wounded	Probably Abu Mus'ab al-Zarqawi	2 suicide car bombs
October 27, 2003	Baghdad	ICRC headquarters, Iraqi police	35 dead, 230+ wounded	Abu Mus'ab al-Zarqawi	5 suicide car bombs
November 12, 2003	An Nasiriyah	Italian military police headquarters	18 Italians and 11 Iraqis dead, 100+ wounded	Abu Mus'ab al-Zarqawi	Suicide truck bomb
November 20, 2003	Kirkuk	Headquarters of Kurdish Patriotic Union of Kurdistan party	5 dead	Probably Ansar al-Islam	Suicide car bomb

DATE(S)	LOCATION	TARGET	CASUALTIES	GROUP	ATTACK METHOD
December 24, 2003	Irbil	Kurdish Interior Ministry building	5 dead, 101 wounded	Probably Ansar al-Islam	Suicide car bomb
December 31, 2003	Baghdad	Nabil restaurant	8 dead, 35 wounded, including 3 *LA Times* journalists	Unknown, possibly Abu Mus'ab al-Zarqawi	Car bomb
January 18, 2004	Baghdad	Main entrance to the Green Zone	31 dead	Probably Abu Mus'ab al-Zarqawi	Suicide car bomb
February 1, 2004	Irbil	Kurdish PUK and KDP party offices	109 dead, 235 wounded	Ansar al-Islam	2 suicide bombers
February 10, 2004	Iskandariyah	Iraqi police station	53 dead	Abu Mus'ab al-Zarqawi	Suicide truck bomb
February 11, 2004	Baghdad	Iraqi police recruitment center	47 dead, 54 wounded	Abu Mus'ab al-Zarqawi	Suicide car bomb
March 2, 2004	Baghdad and Karbala	Shia worshipers during holy day of Ashura	143 dead, 430 wounded	Abu Mus'ab al-Zarqawi	4 suicide bombers
March 17, 2004	Baghdad	Mount Lebanon hotel	29 dead, 50 wounded	Abu Mus'ab al-Zarqawi	Car bomb
April 21, 2004	Basra	Police stations and police academy	74 dead, 94 wounded	Abu Mus'ab al-Zarqawi	5 suicide car bombs
April 24, 2004	Basra	Basra port oil facility	3 dead—2 U.S. Navy, 1 U.S. Coast Guard; 4 U.S. Navy wounded	Abu Mus'ab al-Zarqawi	Gunfire and RPGs from boats

DATE(S)	LOCATION	TARGET	CASUALTIES	GROUP	ATTACK METHOD
May 12, 2004	Iraq	U.S. contractor Nicholas Berg executed	1 dead	Abu Mus'ab al-Zarqawi	Execution
May 17, 2004	Baghdad	Iraqi Governing Council president Ezzedine Salim	8 dead, including Salim	Abu Mus'ab al-Zarqawi	Suicide car bomb
June 17, 2004	Baghdad	Iraqi military recruiting station	35 dead, 138 wounded	Abu Mus'ab al-Zarqawi	Suicide car bomb
June 22, 2004	Iraq	South Korean Kim Sun-Il executed	1 dead	Abu Mus'ab al-Zarqawi	Execution
June 24, 2004	Mosul, Fallujah, Ramadi Iraq	Iraqi police stations and government buildings in several cities	100 dead, 320 wounded	Abu Mus'ab al-Zarqawi	Suicide car bombs
June 28, 2004	Iraq	U.S. Army specialist Keith Maupin executed	1 dead	Unknown, possibly Abu Mus'ab al-Zarqawi	Execution
July 7, 2004	Baghdad	Prime Minister Allawi's office	5 wounded	Abu Mus'ab al-Zarqawi	Mortars
July 14, 2004	Baghdad	Near entrance to the Green Zone	10 dead, 40 wounded, including 1 U.S. soldier	Probably Abu Mus'ab al-Zarqawi	Suicide car bomb
July 28, 2004	Baqubah	Police recruiting center	70 dead, 56 wounded	Probably Abu Mus'ab al-Zarqawi	Suicide car bomb
August 26, 2004	Iraq	Italian journalist Enzo Baldini	1 dead	Probably Abu Mus'ab al-Zarqawi	Execution

DATE(S)	LOCATION	TARGET	CASUALTIES	GROUP	ATTACK METHOD
September 1, 2004	Iraq	12 Nepalese workers	12 dead	Probably Abu Mus'ab al-Zarqawi	Execution
September 12, 2004	Iraq	Turkish truck driver	1 dead	Probably Abu Mus'ab al-Zarqawi	Execution
September 20, 2004	Iraq	American Eugene Armstrong	1 dead	Probably Abu Mus'ab al-Zarqawi	Execution
September 21, 2004	Iraq	American Jack Hensley	1 dead	Probably Abu Mus'ab al-Zarqawi	Execution
REGION: MIDDLE EAST/AFRICA					
April 11, 2002	Djerba, Tunisia	Jewish synagogue	14 German tourists and 6 Tunisians dead; 30+ wounded	Al Qaeda	Suicide truck bomb
May 2002	Morocco	Disrupted plot to bomb U.S. and British warships in the Straits of Gibraltar	—	Al Qaeda; 8 Saudis arrested, including Abu Zubair al-Haili	—
June 2002	Saudi Arabia	Disrupted plot to use SAM against U.S. aircraft at Prince Sultan Airbase	—	Al Qaeda; 13 arrested	—
October 6, 2002	Yemen	French oil tanker *Limburg*	1 dead, 4 wounded	Al Qaeda	Suicide boat attack

DATE(S)	LOCATION	TARGET	CASUALTIES	GROUP	ATTACK METHOD
October 8, 2002	Kuwait	U.S. Marines training for invasion of Iraq on Faylaka Island	2 U.S. Marines dead	Al Qaeda	Gunfire
October 28, 2002	Jordan	Assassination of USAID official Lawrence Foley	1 dead	Abu Mus'ab al-Zarqawi	Gunfire
November 28, 2002	Mombassa, Kenya	Hotel with Israeli tourists, Israeli charter plane	16 dead, including 3 Israelis; 40 wounded, including 18 Israelis	Al Qaeda	Suicide car bomb, 2 failed SAMs launched against charter plane
December 30, 2002	Jiblah, Yemen	Three U.S. Christian missionary doctors at a Southern Baptist hospital	3 dead	Group in Yemen affiliated with al Qaeda	Gunfire
January 21, 2003	Kuwait	Two U.S. contractors	1 dead, 1 wounded	Single Islamic extremist linked to al Qaeda	Gunfire
May 12, 2003	Riyadh, Saudi Arabia	Western housing compounds	35 dead, including 10 Americans and 7 Saudis; 200 wounded	Al Qaeda	3 suicide car bombs
May 16, 2003	Casablanca, Morocco	Western restaurant, Jewish sites, Belgian consulate	44 dead, 100 wounded	Salafi Jihad group affiliated with al Qaeda	Suicide bombers

DATE(S)	LOCATION	TARGET	CASUALTIES	GROUP	ATTACK METHOD
November 8, 2003	Riyadh, Saudi Arabia	Muhaya residential compound	17 dead and 122 wounded, including 4 U.S. wounded	Al Qaeda	Suicide car bomb
November 15, 2003	Istanbul, Turkey	Two Jewish synagogues	25 dead, 300+ wounded	Al Qaeda	2 suicide car bombs
November 20, 2003	Istanbul, Turkey	British Consulate and British HSBC bank	27 dead, 450+ wounded	Al Qaeda	2 suicide car bombs
March 9, 2004	Istanbul, Turkey	Restaurant frequented by freemasons	1 dead, 5 wounded	Al Qaeda	Gunfire
April 21, 2004	Riyadh, Saudi Arabia	Saudi government building	5 dead, 148 wounded	Al Qaeda	Suicide car bomb
April 30, 2004	Amman, Jordan	Disrupted plot to attack Jordan's General Intelligence headquarters, and probably the prime minister's office and U.S. embassy	—	Abu Mus'ab al-Zarqawi; 6 arrested	—
May 1, 2004	Yanbu, Saudi Arabia	Western oil company	5 dead	Islamic extremists	Gunfire
May 29, 2004	Khobar, Saudi Arabia	Housing for Western oil workers	22 dead, of which 3 were Saudi citizens	Al Qaeda	Gunfire
June 6, 2004	Riyadh, Saudi Arabia	BBC reporter Frank Gardner and cameraman Simon Cumbers	1 dead (Cumbers), 1 wounded (Gardner)	Al Qaeda	Gunfire

DATE(S)	LOCATION	TARGET	CASUALTIES	GROUP	ATTACK METHOD
June 8, 2004	Riyadh, Saudi Arabia	U.S. defense contractor Robert Jacobs	1 dead	Al Qaeda	Gunfire
June 12, 2004	Riyadh, Saudi Arabia	U.S. engineer Kenneth Scroggs	1 dead	Al Qaeda	Gunfire
June 18, 2004	Saudi Arabia	U.S. citizen Paul Johnson	1 dead	Al Qaeda	Execution
June 21, 2004	Near Algiers, Algeria	Electrical power plant	11 injured	Salafist Group for Preaching and Combat (GSPC)	Car bomb
September 16, 2004	Riyadh, Saudi Arabia	British citizen Edward Stuart Muirhead-Smith	1 dead	Al Qaeda	Gunfire
September 26, 2004	Jiddah, Saudi Arabia	French citizen Laurent Barbot	1 dead	Al Qaeda	Gunfire
REGION: EUROPE/RUSSIA/EURASIA					
December 22, 2001	American Airlines flight from Paris to Miami	Disrupted plot to blow up airplane using a shoe bomb by Richard Reid	—	Al Qaeda; 1 arrest	—
April 23, 2002	Germany	Arrests of 9 Islamic extremist members of al-Tawhid; support cell for al Qaeda in South Asia	—	Al Qaeda-linked al-Tawhid movement	—

DATE(S)	LOCATION	TARGET	CASUALTIES	GROUP	ATTACK METHOD
October 23–26, 2002	Moscow, Russia	Hostage taking of 700+ at theater	41 extremists and 129 hostages dead	Chechen extremists linked to al Qaeda	Hostage taking
November 9, 2002	London, UK	Disrupted plot to target probably the London subway system	—	Al Qaeda; 6 arrested	—
December 27, 2002	Grozny, Chechnya	Headquarters of Russian-backed Chechen government	80 dead	Chechen extremists linked to al Qaeda	Suicide truck bomb
December 24–27, 2002	Paris, France	Disrupted plot to attack Russian Embassy	—	North African extremists with links to Chechen extremists and al Qaeda; 9 arrested	—
January 5, 2003	London, UK	Disrupted ricin plot, unknown targets	—	Al Qaeda; 8 arrested	—
January 22, 2003	Near Venice, Italy	Disrupted plot to attack NATO base in Verona, Italy	—	Islamic extremists linked to al Qaeda; 5 arrested	—
January 24, 2003	Madrid, Spain	Unknown, associated with disrupted ricin plot	—	Al Qaeda-associated North Africans; 16 arrested	—

DATE(S)	LOCATION	TARGET	CASUALTIES	GROUP	ATTACK METHOD
May 8(?), 2003	Kyrgyzstan	Disrupted plot to bomb the U.S. Embassy and hotel in Bishkek	—	Islamic Movement of Uzbekistan	—
May 12, 2003	Znamenskoye, Chechnya	Government building	59 dead, dozens wounded	Chechen extremists linked to al Qaeda	Suicide truck bomb
May 14, 2003	Ilishkhan Yurt, Chechnya	Attempted assassination of President Akhmad Kadyrov at a religious festival	18 dead, 145 wounded	Chechen extremists linked to al Qaeda	Suicide bomber
June 5, 2003	Mozdok, Russia	Bus carrying military personnel	16 dead	Chechen extremists linked to al Qaeda	Female suicide bomber
July 5, 2003	Moscow, Russia	Music concert at Tushino airfield	16 dead	Chechen extremists linked to al Qaeda	2 female suicide bombers
August 1, 2003	Mozdok, Russia	Military hospital	50 dead, 77 wounded	Chechen extremists linked to al Qaeda	Suicide car bomb
September 3, 2003	Southern Russia	Commuter train	5 dead, 11 wounded	Chechen extremists linked to al Qaeda	Bomb

DATE(S)	LOCATION	TARGET	CASUALTIES	GROUP	ATTACK METHOD
September 16, 2003	Southern Russia	Government Security Services building	3 dead, 25 wounded	Chechen extremists linked to al Qaeda	Suicide truck bomb
December 5, 2003	Southern Russia	Commuter train	44 dead, 150 wounded	Chechen extremists linked to al Qaeda	Suicide bomber
December 9, 2003	Moscow, Russia	National Hotel	6 dead	Chechen extremists linked to al Qaeda	Female suicide bomber
February 6, 2004	Moscow, Russia	Moscow subway	41 dead, approximately 100 wounded	Chechen extremists linked to al Qaeda	Bomb
March 11, 2004	Madrid, Spain	Commuter trains	191 dead, 1,900+ wounded	Moroccan extremist linked to al Qaeda	Bombs
March 31, 2004	London, UK	Disrupted plot to use osmium tetroxide bomb	—	Al Qaeda; 9 arrested	—
March 28–30, 2004	Tashkent, Uzbekistan	Uzbek government buildings, and possibly the U.S. Embassy and an airbase used by the U.S.	42 dead, 31 wounded	Islamic Movement of Uzbekistan	Suicide bombers, some female

DATE(S)	LOCATION	TARGET	CASUALTIES	GROUP	ATTACK METHOD
May 9, 2004	Grozny, Chechnya	President Akhmad Kadyrov	24 dead, including Kadyrov	Chechen extremists linked to al Qaeda	Bomb
June 9, 2004	Milan, Italy	Disrupted plot to possibly bomb Paris subway system; led to Belgian arrest of 15 associated with plot	—	Egyptian extremist and plot mastermind Rabei Osman Sayed Ahmed arrested	—
June 15, 2004	Paris, France	Disrupted plot to possibly bomb Paris subway system	—	Islamic extremists; 12 arrested	—
June 22, 2004	Nazran, Ingushetia Province, Russia	Interior Ministry buildings	92 dead, 120 wounded	Chechen extremists linked to al Qaeda	Gunfire and RPGs
July 13, 2004	Grozny, Chechnya	Failed attempt to assassinate Acting President Sergei Abramov in his motorcade	1 dead, 3 wounded	Unknown	Bomb
July 30, 2004	Tashkent, Uzbekistan	U.S. Embassy, Israeli Embassy, Uzbek prosecutor's office	4 dead, 1 wounded	Islamic Movement of Uzbekistan	3 suicide bombers
August 25, 2004	Russia	Two Russian airliners crash after explosions	90 dead	Chechen extremists	Probably one female suicide bomber on each plane

DATE(S)	LOCATION	TARGET	CASUALTIES	GROUP	ATTACK METHOD
August 31, 2004	Moscow, Russia	Russian subway station	9 dead	Chechen extremists	Female suicide bomber
September 1–3, 2004	Beslan, Russia	Hostage taking of school building	350+ dead, 650+ wounded	Chechen extremists	Gunfire and explosives
REGION: SOUTH ASIA					
January 22, 2002	Calcutta, India	U.S. Consulate, Calcutta annex; press, cultural, and public affairs offices	5 dead, 16 wounded (no U.S. citizens)	Lashkar-e-Tayyiba	Drive-by shooting on motorcycle
January 31, 2002	Karachi, Pakistan	U.S. jounalist Daniel Pearl	1 dead	Al Qaeda	Execution
March 17, 2002	Islamabad, Pakistan	Protestant International Church	5 dead, including 2 U.S.; 46 wounded, including 13 U.S.	Lashkar-e-Tayyiba	Grenade attack
May 8, 2002	Karachi, Pakistan	Pakistani Navy shuttle bus	12 dead, including 11 French; 19 wounded, including 11 French	Al Qaeda	Suicide car bomb
June 14, 2002	Karachi, Pakistan	U.S. Consulate, Karachi	11 dead; 51 wounded, including 1 U.S. and 1 Japanese citizen	Al Qaeda	Suicide car bomb
July 8, 2002	Kabul, Afghanistan	Assassination of Afghan Vice President Haji Abdul Qadir	2 dead, including Qadir	Unknown, possibly al Qaeda or Taliban	Gunfire

DATE(S)	LOCATION	TARGET	CASUALTIES	GROUP	ATTACK METHOD
July 30, 2002	Kabul, Afghanistan	Disrupted plot to attack government officials, buildings	—	Al Qaeda; 1 Arab arrested with car bomb	—
September 5, 2002	Qandahar, Afghanistan	Failed assassination attempted against President Karzai	1 U.S. military and 1 Afghan wounded	Al Qaeda	Gunfire
September 5, 2002	Kabul, Afghanistan	Afghan commercial market	30 dead, 150 wounded	Al Qaeda or Gulbuddin Hekmatyar	Car bomb
September 11, 2002	Kashmir, India	Law Minister Mushtaq Ahmed Lone	7 (Lone and 6 security guards)	Probably Lashkar-e-Tayyiba	Gunfire
January 31, 2003	Qandahar, Afghanistan	Bus carrying civilians	18 dead, 2 wounded	Al Qaeda, Taliban or Gulbuddin Hekmatyar	Bomb
June 7, 2003	Eastern Afghanistan	Bus carrying German soldiers	5 dead, including 4 Germans; 31 wounded Germans	Al Qaeda	Suicide car bomb
August 25, 2003	Mumbai (Bombay), India	Commercial district near Consulate Mumbai	52 dead, 153 wounded	Lashkar-e-Tayyiba	2 car bombs
December 25, 2003	Rawalpindi, Pakistan	Failed assassination attempt against President Musharraf	14 dead, 46 wounded;a 12/14/2003 assassination attempt resulted in no casualties	Pakistani Islamic extremists linked to al Qaeda	2 truck bombs

DATE(S)	LOCATION	TARGET	CASUALTIES	GROUP	ATTACK METHOD
March 2, 2004	Quetta, Pakistan	Shia worshipers during holy day of Ashura	51 dead, 154 wounded	Lashkar-e-Jhangvi	Gunfire, grenades
May 3, 2004	Gawadar, Pakistan	Chinese engineers	3 dead (all Chinese), 11 wounded	Pakistani Islamic extremists	Car bomb
May 26, 2004	Karachi, Pakistan	Pakistani–American Cultural Center	1 dead, 25 wounded	Pakistani Islamic extremists	2 car bombs
June 11, 2004	Karachi, Pakistan	Failed assassination attempt against V Corps General Ahsan Saleem Hayat	6 dead, 10 wounded	Pakistani Sunni extremists, possibly linked to al Qaeda	Gunfire and improvised explosive device
July 30, 2004	Fateh Jang, North Pakistan	Failed assassination attempt against Minister of Finance and PM candidate Shauket Aziz	22 dead, 22 wounded	Pakistani extremists	Suicide bomber
August 29, 2004	Kabul, Afghanistan	Dyncorp training headquarters for Afghan military	9 dead, including 3 Americans; 1 American wounded	Taliban	Suicide car bomb
September 20, 2004	Takhar Province, Afghanistan	Failed assassination attempt on Afghan VP Nayiamatullah Shahrani	1 injured	Taliban or al Qaeda	Roadside bomb

Date(s)	Location	Target	Casualties	Group	Attack Method
Region: Southeast Asia					
December 20, 2001	Singapore	Disrupted plot to bomb the U.S., UK, Israeli, and Australian embassies	—	Al Qaeda and Jemaah Islamiya; 33 arrested	—
April 22, 2002	General Santos City, Philippines	Shopping mall	15 dead, 70 wounded	Abu Sayyaf Group	3 bombs
September, 2002	Philippines	Disrupted plot to assassinate President Arroyo	—	Jemaah Islamiya; 4 arrested	—
October 2, 2002	Zamboanga, Philippines	U.S. military at restaurant near their base	1 dead, 1 wounded—U.S. soldiers	Jemaah Islamiya	Bomb
October 10, 2002	Kidapawan, southern Philippines	Bus stop	6 dead, 10 wounded	Possibly Jemaah Islamiya	Bomb
October 12, 2002	Bali, Indonesia	Nightclubs frequented by Westerners	202 dead, including 88 Australians and 7 U.S.; 300+ wounded	Jemaah Islamiya	2 car bombs
October 17, 2002	Zamboanga, Philippines	Shopping district in city	6 dead, approximately 150 wounded	Jemaah Islamiya	2 bombs
October 18, 2002	Manila, Philippines	Civilian bus	3 dead, 22 wounded	Possibly Jemaah Islamiya	Bomb

Date(s)	Location	Target	Casualties	Group	Attack Method
December 26, 2002	Zamboanga del Norte, Philippines	Filipinos employed by Canadian Toronto Ventures, Inc., Pacific mining company	13 killed, 10 wounded	Moro Islamic Liberation Front (MILF)	Gunfire
March 4, 2003	Davao City, southern Philippines	Davao airport and wharf	23 dead, including 1 U.S. citizen; 146 wounded	Abu Sayyaf Group	Bomb
June 2003	Thailand	Disrupted plot to attack several Western embassies and tourist sites	—	Jemaah Islamiya	—
August 5, 2003	Jakarta, Indonesia	Marriott hotel	13 dead, 149 wounded	Jemaah Islamiya	Suicide car bomb
June 29, 2004	Manila, Philippines	Disrupted plot to assassinate President Arroyo during inauguration ceremonies	—	Jemaah Islamiya; 6 arrested	—
September 9, 2004	Jakarta, Indonesia	Road outside the Australian Embassy	8 dead, 182 wounded	Jemaah Islamiya	Suicide car bomb

Notes

Chapter 4

1. In Bahrain, the ascension of Shaykh Hamad bin 'Isa al Khalifah in 1999 marked the fourth occasion on which the eldest son succeeded his father as emir. Similarly, in Qatar, Shaykh Khalifah al Thani seized power by deposing his cousin in 1972. Khalifah was followed by his son in June 1995, who consequently named his own son, Jasim, as heir apparent. Abu Dhabi also holds to the pattern. As Sultan Qabus bin Sa'id has no offspring, Oman remains the only Gulf state without an heir apparent. See, e.g., J. E. Peterson, "Succession in the States of the Gulf Cooperation Council," *Washington Quarterly* 24(4) (August 2001): 173–86.

2. The notion of a "military-mullah alliance" is taken from the International Crisis Group, "Pakistan: The Mullahs and the Military," *ICG Asia Report No. 49,* March 20, 2003.

3. International Crisis Group, "Pakistan: Madrasas, Extremism and the Military," ICG Asia Report No. 36, July 29, 2002: 20–21.

4. Ibid., 20.

Chapter 5

1. Shibley Telhami, "A View from the Arab World: A Survey in Five Countries," Brookings Institution, March 13, 2003.

2. Pew Research Center for People and the Press, "Pew Global Attitudes Project: Wave 2 Update Survey (2003)" (April/May 2003).

3. Marc Lynch, "Taking Arabs Seriously," *Foreign Affairs* (September/October 2003).

4. Kim Cragin et al., *Strategic Influence Policy* (Santa Monica, CA: Rand, forthcoming 2004), p. 6.

5. Edward Djerejian et al., "Changing Minds Winning Peace: A New Strategic Direction for U.S. Public Diplomacy in the Arab and Muslim World," October 1, 2003.

6. Cragin, *Strategic Influence Policy.*

7. For example, the promotion of human rights in the context of the prisoner abuse scandal at Abu Ghraib.

8. President Bush acknowledged as much in a November 2003 speech, noting that "we must shake off decades of failed policy in the Middle East. Your nation and mine, in the past, have been willing to make a bargain, to tolerate oppression for the sake of stability. Longstanding ties often led us to overlook the faults of local elites," available online at http://www.whitehouse.gov/news/releases/2003/11/20031119-1.html.

9. CNN/*USA Today*/Gallup, "Nationwide Poll of Iraq: Final Topline," March 22–April 9, 2004.

10. BBC, "Iraqi Media Test New Environment," June 29, 2004.

11. In November 2003, the Iraqi Governing Council temporarily banned al-Arabiya from broadcasting in Iraq and seized its equipment in Baghdad. In August 2004, the Iraqi government announced it would shut down al-Jazeera's Baghdad bureau for thirty days.

12. Adapted from a table appearing in GAO, "U.S. International Broadcasting: Challenges Facing the Broadcasting Board of Governors," GAO-04-711T, April 29, 2004.

13. Broadcasting Board of Governors, "Alhurra and Radio Sawa: Progress Report," April 2004 data compiled by ACNielsen in April 2004 for all countries excluding Qatar. Qatar data were compiled in a similar telephone survey conducted in August 2003. The survey group was limited to adults fifteen years or older. The sample size was 5,737 adults. "Weekly listeners" refers to those who listened to Radio Sawa at least once in the previous week. "Reliability" refers to those who agreed that Radio Sawa's news was "very or somewhat reliable."

14. Ibid.

15. Alan Sipress, "For Many Iraqis, U.S.-Backed TV Echoes the Voice of Its Sponsor; Station Staffers Acknowledge Their Reluctance to Criticize," *Washington Post,* January 8, 2004.

16. Terrestrial transmission allows non-satellite ready households in Iraq to view al-Hurra via Channel 12 in Baghdad and Channel 3 in Basra; BBC, "Iraq/USA: Survey of U.S.-funded al-Hurra TV's Audience," July 21, 2004.

17. GAO, "U.S. International Broadcasting: Challenges Facing the Broadcasting Board of Governors," GAO-04-711T, April 29, 2004, p. 9.

18. Broadcasting Board of Governors, "Alhurra and Radio Sawa: Progress Report," April 2004.

19. Ibid.

20. Ibid.

21. Pew Research Center for People and the Press, "Pew Global Attitudes Project."

22. Ibid.
23. Telhami, "A View from the Arab World."
24. Available online at http://www.whitehouse.gov/news/releases/2003/11/20031119-1.html.
25. Prompting David Frum to ask, "Why Won't You Listen When We Tell You What You Want to Hear," *Daily Telegraph,* November 20, 2003.

CHAPTER 7

1. GAO, March 2003; Democratic Members of the House Select Committee on Homeland Security, America at Risk, January 2004; *Richmond Times Dispatch,* March 23, 2003.
2. National Emergency Managers Association, "State Spending and Homeland Security Funds," April 2, 2003.

CHAPTER 8

1. Dana Priest, "Tenet Warns of Al Qaeda Threat," *Washington Post,* February 25, 2004.
2. Kamran Khan and Molly Moore, "Two Nuclear Experts Briefed Bin Laden, Pakistanis Say," *Washington Post,* December 12, 2001.
3. Israr Ahmad, "The Rationale of Islamic Jihad." Available online at http://www.the-quest.info/viewpoint/.
4. Kamran Khan, "Pakistan Releases Nuclear Scientists for Ramadan's End," *Washington Post,* December 16, 2001.
5. President George W. Bush, "Remarks by the President in the Rose Garden," The White House, December 20, 2001.
6. Graham Allison, *Nuclear Terrorism: The Ultimate Preventable Catastrophe* (New York: Times Books, 2004).
7. Ibid.
8. Available online at http://www.nti.org/db/nisprofs/russia/weapons/tacnukes/97nums.htm.
9. Interview on *Meet the Press,* December 15, 1991.
10. Ibid.
11. "Russia Sends Troops to Guard Nuclear Sites," Reuters (Moscow) September 1, 2004.
12. Gary Samore, "North Korea's Weapons Programme: A Net Assessment," *International Institute for Strategic Studies,* January 21, 2004.

13. Available online at http://www.cfr.org/campaign2004/issue_brief.php?issue=14.

14. The 9/11 Commission Report, p. xx.

15. "Bush's Nuclear Insights," *Boston Globe,* February 16, 2004.

16. Robert Walpole, CIA national intelligence officer for strategic and nuclear programs, in testimony to the Senate, March 11, 2001.

CHAPTER 9

1. Robert E. Ebel, "The National Security Implications of Oil" (speech, The Wilmington Club, Wilmington, DE, May 25, 1999).

2. Ibid.

3. Natural Resources Defense Fund, available online at http://www.nrdf.com.

4. John Carey, "Kerry's High-Wattage Energy Plan," *Business Week,* August 9, 2004.

5. BP, Year in Review, 2003, available online at http://www.bp.com/sectiongenericarticle.do?categoryId=760&contentId=2014223.

6. Michelle Billig, "Issue Brief: Energy," Council on Foreign Relations, August 2004, available online at http://www.cfr.org/campaign2004/issue_brief.php?issue=03.

7. "Security of Oil Supply; Saudi Oil Comes Under Threat," *Petroleum Economist,* July 13, 2004.

8. Ibid.

9. "Where Oil Is King: Russia Overtakes Saudi Arabia as World's Leading Oil Producer" *Jane's Foreign Report,* Issue 2682-28, March 2002.

10. "Gazpromotion," *Economist,* September 16, 2004.

Additional Sources

Local Newspapers Consulted

Al-Ahram
Al-Sha'ab
Al-Wafd
Cairo Times
Egypt Today

Books and Periodicals

Abdalla, Ahmed. "Egypt's Islamists and the State: From Complicity to Confrontation." *Middle East Report* 183. July 1993.

———. "Mubarak's Gamble." *Middle East Report* 168. January 1991.

Abdo, Genevieve. "Media and Information: The Case of Iran." *Social Research* 70.3. Fall 2003.

———. "Iran's Generation of Outsiders." *Washington Quarterly* 24.4. August 2001.

———. "The Fragility of Khatami's Revolution." *Washington Quarterly* 23.4. August 2000.

Ackerman, Spencer, et al. "Pakistan for Bush. July Surprise?" *The New Republic.* July 19, 2004.

Ajami, Fouad. "The Sorrows of Egypt." *Foreign Affairs* 74. September 1995. 72–88.

Allison, Graham. *Nuclear Terrorism: The Ultimate Preventable Catastrophe.* New York: Times Books, 2004.

Al-Rasheed, Madawi. *A History of Saudi Arabia.* Cambridge: Cambridge University Press, 2002.

Alterman, Jon B. "Egypt: Stable, but for How Long?" *Washington Quarterly* 23.4. August 2000.

Baer, Robert. "The Fall of the House of Saud." *Atlantic Monthly* 29.4. May 2003. 53–62.

Bahgat, Gawdat. "The New Iran: A Myth or a Reality?" *Asian Affairs* 29.2. June 1998.

Bakhash, Shaul. "Reformists, Conservatives, and Iran's 2000 Parlimentary Elections." In *Iran, Iraq, and the Arab Gulf States,* edited by Joseph Kechichian. New York: Palgrave, 2001.

Campagna, Joel. "From Accommodation to Confrontation: The Muslim Brotherhood in the Mubarak Years." *Journal of International Affairs* 50. Summer 1996. 278–304.

Codevilla, Angelo. "Heresy and History." *The American Spectator* 37.4. May 2004. 22–28.

Cordesman, Anthony. *Saudi Arabia Enters the Twenty-First Century: The Military and International Security Dimensions.* Washington, D.C.: CSIS, 2003.

Council on Foreign Relations. "Emergency Responders: Drastically Underfunded, Dangerously Unprepared." Report of an Independent Task Force, Sponsored by the Council on Foreign Relations. New York: CFR, 2003.

———. "Terrorist Financing." Report of an Independent Task Force, Sponsored by the Council on Foreign Relations. New York: CFR, 2002.

De Bellaigue, Christopher. "Iran's Last Chance for Reform?" *Washington Quarterly* 24.4. August 2001.

Doran, Michael. "The Saudi Paradox." *Foreign Affairs* 83.1. January/February 2004. 35–51.

Ehteshami, Anoushiravan. "Iran's International Posture After the Fall of Baghdad." *Middle East Journal* 58.2. Spring 2004.

Esposito, John L., and R. K. Ramazani, eds. *Iran at the Crossroads.* New York: Palgrave, 2001.

Fandy, Mamoun. *Saudi Arabia and the Politics of Dissent.* New York: St. Martin's, 1999.

Flynn, Stephen. *America the Vulnerable: How Our Government Is Failing to Protect Us from Terrorism.* New York: HarperCollins, 2004.

Geiger, Keri. "Pakistan: The Road to Recovery." *AsiaMoney* 15.2. March 20, 2004.

Haqqani, Husain. "Islam's Medieval Outposts." *Foreign Policy* 133. November 2002.

Hashim, Ahmed. "Civil–Military Relations in the Islamic Republic of Iran." In *Iran, Iraq, and the Arab Gulf States,* edited by Joseph Kechichian. New York: Palgrave, 2001.

Hassan, Nasra. "Al-Qaeda's Understudy." *Atlantic Monthly* 293.5. June 2004.

Hendriks, Bertus. "Egypt's Elections, Mubarak's Bind." *MERIP Reports* 129. January 1985.

International Crisis Group. "Pakistan: The Mullahs and the Military." *ICG Asia Report No. 49*. Islamabad/Brussels. March 20, 2003.

———. "Madrassas, Extremism, and the Military." *ICG Asia Report No. 36*. Islamabad/Brussels. July 29, 2002.

Kechichian, Joseph. *Succession in Saudi Arabia*. New York: Palgrave, 2001.

Kechichian, Joseph, ed. *Iran, Iraq, and the Arab Gulf States*. New York: Palgrave, 2001.

Khalidi, Omar. "Mawlana Mawdudi and the Future Political Order in British India." *Muslim World* 93.3/4. Summer 2003.

Kienle, Eberhard. *A Grand Delusion: Democracy and Economic Reform in Egypt*. London: I.B. Tauris, 2001.

Lidstone, Digby. "Special Report Saudi Arabia." *Middle East Economic Digest* 46. 2002.

Mason, Whit. "Iran's Simmering Discontent." World Policy Journal 19.1. Spring 2002.

Milani, Mohsen M. "Reform and Resistance in the Islamic Republic." In *Iran at the Crossroads,* edited by John L. Esposito and R. K. Ramazani. New York: Palgrave, 2001.

Najjar, Fauzi. "Book Banning in Contemporary Egypt." *Muslim World* 91.3/4. Fall 2001.

Obaid, Nawaf. "In Al-Saud We Trust." *Foreign Policy* 128. Jan/Feb 2002. 72–74.

Peterson, J.E. "Succession in the States of the Gulf Cooperation Council." *Washington Quarterly* 24.4. August 2001. 173–186.

Pfeffer, Anshel. "The Last Pharaoh." *Jerusalem Post*. 9 July 2004.

Post, Erika. "Egypt's Elections." *MERIP Middle East Report* 147. July 1987.

Posusney, Marsha. "Behind the Ballot Box: Electoral Engineering in the Arab World." *Middle East Report* 209. Winter 1998.

Remnick, David. "Going Nowhere." *The New Yorker*. 21 July 2004.

Rouleau, Eric. "Trouble in the Kingdom." *Foreign Affairs* 81.4. Summer 2002. 75–89.

Roy, Olivier. "Tensions and Options Among the Iranian Clerical Establishment." In *Iran, Iraq, and the Arab Gulf States,* edited by Joseph Kechichian. New York: Palgrave, 2001.

Ryan, Curtis. "Political Strategies and Regime Survival in Egypt." *Journal of Third World Studies* 18.2. Fall 2001. 25–46.

Sachedina, Abdulaziz. "The Rule of the Religious Jurist in Iran." In *Iran at the Crossroads,* edited by John L. Esposito and R. K. Ramazani. New York: Palgrave, 2001.

Talwar, Puneet. "Iran in the Balance." *Foreign Affairs* 80.4. July 2001.

Singer, P.W. "Pakistan's Madrassahs: Ensuring a System of Education not Jihad." Brookings Institution. Analysis Paper #14. November 2001.

Stern, Jessica. "Pakistan's Jihad Culture." *Foreign Affairs* 79.6. November 2000.

Weaver, Mary Anne. "Pharaohs-in-Waiting." *Atlantic Monthly* 292.3. October 2003.

Wickham, Carrie R. *Mobilizing Islam: Religion, Activism, and Political Change in Egypt.* New York: Columbia University Press, 2002.